CW00548861

Border Voices

on
SCOTTISH BORDERS
and BEYOND

An Anthology from
Borders Writers' Forum

Edited by Dorothy Bruce

*Cover photograph - Chinese junk in Eyemouth Harbour
with Gunsgreen House in background.*

This anthology is a taster of the writing of members of Borders Writers' Forum on the theme of Scottish Borders and Beyond

Edited by Dorothy Bruce

Further information on the Forum and its members can be found at
www.borderswritersforum.org

Border Voices on Scottish Borders and Beyond: An Anthology from Borders Writers' Forum
Copyright ©Borders Writers' Forum, October 2012.

British Library Cataloguing-in-Publication Data
A CIP catalogue record for this book is available from the British Library

Paperback ISBN 978-0-9567128-1-3
Hardback   ISBN 978-0-9567128-2-0

Published by
Borders Writers' Forum
Kirkcairn
Westruther
Gordon
Scottish Borders TD3 6NE
www.borderswritersforum.org

This publication is supported by the Creative Arts Business Network (CABN). CABN is part of the South of Scotland Creative Enterprise Initiative funded by Creative Scotland, LEADER and Scottish Borders Council.

Printed and bound by Think Ink Ltd, 11-13 Phillip Road, Ipswich, Suffolk IP2 8BH

Border Voices

on **SCOTTISH BORDERS AND BEYOND**

Foreword by Professor Ian Campbell, Emeritus Professor of Scottish and Victorian Literature at the University of Edinburgh

Border Voices – on Scottish Borders and Beyond. And Beyond indeed. Border Voices walks a tightrope from beginning to end, its footwork deftly balancing the local with the universal: there's a very apt quotation from Mahatma Gandhi to the effect that "I do not want my house to be walled in on all sides and my windows to be stuffed. I want the cultures of all the lands to be blown about my house as freely as possible." Blowing about the mind is what these stories, poems, illustrations, accounts of real life do to the reader. Another very apt quotation from a poem this time, the writer speaking of

Clicking the digital camera
Of my mind
Telling tales
Of a less hurried landscape.
Thinking.
This is the life. It's good to be a writer.

The image is one that could be sustained through this book with its kaleidoscope of subjects, anchored to Border experience, but as comfortable in the Himalaya as in the familiar realities of a Border landscape where history is alive. When one writer recalls that "Father Wallace had gone to his Maker by way of Huntly, Douay, Valladolid and Traquair", the list simply underlines the open-ness of mind and imagination which makes this book, prose and poetry, such an explosion of experience from the Borders outward.

That explosion gathers force from the writing festivals and gatherings which increasingly punctuate the year, and it is good to see the energy of these occasions tapped and here preserved for leisurely reading. The energy of Borders writing obviously ripples out beyond any obvious horizon. Long may it do so.

Ian Campbell   21 September 2012

Costume on display in the entrance hall of
The Haining, Selkirk.
www.thehaining.co.uk

Border Voices

on SCOTTISH BORDERS and BEYOND

Illness and the Child Open Writing Competition

In 2012 Borders Writers' Forum held an open writing competition in aid of the Sick Kids Friends Foundation. Judges were Ron Butlin, prize-winning novelist and poet, for poetry, and Professor Ian Campbell, Emeritus Professor of Scottish and Victorian Literature at the University of Edinburgh, for prose entries.

Winners were **Fiona Colton**, (Poetry) from Selkirk, and **David Allen** (Prose) from London who were presented at an event at the Borders Book Festival in June with a specially commissioned piece of glass from Scottish Borders Art Glass in Hawick.

Last Chips in Eyemouth

Poem by *Arthur Parsons*

We sat sea staring, not wanting to go.
The all embracing tidal flow
Slapped the cracked muddy creeks
Scrubbing their crabby cheeks
Under the blind portholed gaze
Of wind bobbed boats, all ablaze
With the day's last bloodied light
As the dying sun drowned in the night.

Tangled white yachts, moored in rope knitting,
Groaned their varnished decks, rattled their rigging,
Wanting away from others' proximity,
Trying to assert their marine femininity.
Dora, Flora and Mistress Penelope,
Longing to be freed from their chains on the Quay;
To be bathed, held and caressed
By the sea's foam-fingered crests.

But we are like lovers, harbour-promenading,
Who slow their shuffling steps, to delay a parting,
Hoping the last lingered kiss won't come.
This town with its plastic flotsam and jetsam,
Its cans and bottles and tattooed bums,
Battered straw hats and tyre-bellied mums
Anchors with memories of cuddles and smiles
On talk-walked beaches for steep-cliffed miles.

Our time here's expired, another place calls
With screeching brake-pads not wheeling seagulls
The daily drudge of salaried endeavour
Unaffected by tides, inclement weather
Or the muscular ripples of planetary power
Ruled instead by banks in high-rise towers,
Where we'll sail by, as the salt wind screams,
Battening hatches, walking secure in our dreams.

Fiction by *Margaret Skea*

Working Away

Margaret Skea's story *Working Away* was the Adult Prose and Overall Winner of the 2011 Neil Gunn Award.

The agency man is talking, insistent as a mosquito. 'This is how it will be. Where you will go. Very nice people. Very good room. It will be very fine.' Mmberane pauses, curious only. He notes the dark suit, the crisp, white shirt, and reaches for his own, newly bought handkerchief, shaking it out and raising it to his brow. The feel of the stiff cotton sings to him: Today I have begun.

*   *   *   *   *

On the brow of the hill he stops, breathing deeply, and again mops his forehead, the handkerchief already limp. Below him the village slumbers, the contours softened by the heat, the cluster of circular huts mud-brown daubs against the smear of earth and sky. In the corner of his eye he catches a streak of yellow followed by red, a shout, a tumble, high-pitched laughter carried to him in the still air. He lifts his bag, empty now but for the roll of sacking and his money purse, and slings it over his shoulder, his chest swelling at the clink of coins.

Iminza has seen him and comes running, her dress lifting and spinning as she leaps up and wraps her legs and arms around him. Saliku tugs at his trouser leg, poking a stubby finger through the hole at the back of the knee.

'Aaie!' Mmberane shifts Iminza onto one hip, bends and swings Saliku up onto the other, presses them close, tells them, 'Daddy has sold every-thing today.' He bounces them up and down as he strides along the track, so that they squeal and cling tight. It is mid-afternoon, the village quiet, almost deserted. Only the old remain, resting in the shade of their huts, and those of the children either too young or too poor to go to school. He knows the talk: that he will never amount to anything, that Grace made a mistake in marrying him, and feels a stab of regret: he should have lingered, come home late when all would see the empty sack, his bulging purse.

He is kneeling by the bed dragging out the carved box that lies beneath, as Grace enters. She stops, and sensing in her stillness the apprehension that she is too loyal to express, he beams reassurance, holds out the purse.

'Ninety shillings.'

'I thought...' She weighs the purse in her hand, her dark eyes damp, and he reaches for her, buries her face in his chest, leans his chin on the tight fuzz of her hair.

'This year' he says, 'This year we will be fine.' His finger traces the line of her spine, comes to rest in the small of her back. 'I feel it.'

The next day is good also, and the next, and each night as Grace curves into him, welcoming, he responds without reserve. It is three o'clock on Friday when he makes his last sale: to a woman in a mission handout, the pattern faded under the armpits, one mismatched button on the front. He has six potatoes left and she hesitates, puts her hand in her pocket as if counting the coins there, before holding out her string bag,

'Four,' she says, her chin tilting.

He pops them in, asks for seven shillings, and as he waits, sees Grace in a similar dress, though her hem never drags. 'Here,' he thrusts the remaining two potatoes into the bag, avoids her eyes, fans his face, 'Aaie...it is too hot and who would want only two?'

He brushes away her mumbled 'Asante' embarrassed by her thanks, and stretches, rolling up the sacking, tucking it under his arm as he drifts around the market stalls. Many things tempt him, yet each time he pauses he jingles the money in his purse, looks, shakes his head; passes on. It is a fine thing to be able to choose not to buy. He lingers longest under a sign proclaiming 'The best batik-maker in Serem'. The stall-holder unfurls the fabric with a practised tug, the colours blending and swirling before him. Stroking the bright cottons he imagines Grace: the pattern cascading from her shoulder, over her breasts, cradling her smooth, slightly rounded stomach, the curve of her thighs. He reaches for his purse, hesitates, blurts out,

'Next month...my wife... it is her birthday - I will come then.'

The agency man is there again, in the corner where the stalls peter out into an open area cluttered with ancient bicycles, rickety ox-carts and the occasional dented van. This time he stands one foot on the runner of a gleaming matatu; his vowels stretched, sinuous.

'Very good hotel. Very good tips. It will be very fine.'

A man steps forward and hands over a clutch of notes before swinging his bag onto the minibus roof rack and joining those already seated inside. Watching, Mmberane thinks of how the man will come home only twice or three times a year, that his children will be strangers to him, and is glad that he himself has no schooling, no certificate.

*   *   *   *   *

Grace is cross-legged on the floor, a dress for Iminza spread on her lap, a handful of pins sticking from her mouth. She is pressing the fabric with her fingers, smoothing out the gathers around the waist, pinning, tucking. It is a pretty dress of turquoise satin, embroidered flowers scattered across the skirt, but Mmberane brushes it aside, gently removes the pins from her lips, cradles her hands, elation in his voice.

'This week, two hundred and eighty shillings. Next month,' he squeezes her fingers, 'the beans will be ready and who knows...' He picks up the dress, closes his hand over the label at the neck, hiding the English name in faded ink. 'Soon,' he says, 'Soon I will buy new.' Grace leans into him and he feels her heartbeat, and lower down another flutter. He rocks back, searches her face, sees the hope shining.

'I wasn't sure. Not till today. But I think we will be blessed again.' For a moment a shadow crosses her face. 'If all is well.'

He rests his hand on her stomach, 'It will be. It will be very well.'

*   *   *   *   *

He carries the beans to market, a swing in his step. His usual pitch is taken, but he finds a space, stretching out his sacking, setting up the scales, lining up the stones as weights. On one side of him an old woman, as scrawny as the three chickens that squawk and peck in a crate at her feet, and on the other, a man with his head bent over a whetstone, feeling for the edge, the knife in his hand sliding and lifting, sliding and lifting in continuous motion.

From the woman Mmberane's 'Jambo' elicits a toothless smile, deepening the creases in her face, while the knife-sharpener tilts his head towards the voice, his eyes opaque as an overcast sky. Mmberane shifts on his haunches, makes a surreptitious sign of the cross, but stays his ground. Afterwards, walking home as the heat bleeds out of the sun, he dismisses the superstition and instead blames the good harvest, the many other bean-sellers, that a third of his crop lies limp in his bag, that his purse is light.

The next day he leaves before dawn to claim a different pitch, prays his luck will change. But though it is not a bad week, it is not a good one either, and each evening he hurries past the batik stall, head down, reminding himself that there are still two weeks until Grace's birthday. At the foot of the market he skirts the perimeter to avoid the accusing line of girl's dresses strung out like gaily-coloured flags.

But he cannot avoid the agency man, persuading his clients into the comfort of the matatu, his voice repetitive as a recording. '...Where you will go...What you will do. Very good people...It will be very fine.' Unable to resist Mmberane stops, watches the flash of gold in his mouth, listens. Sees the pictures: summer-bright, many-coloured, like finest batik.

*   *   *   *   *

He has almost decided, but has given himself one last day. It is cooler now and though there are people enough, few stop, those who do buying little, haggling hard. He must carry many things away again and when they have paid for the school for Mbone there will be less in the box, not more.

Afterwards, when he has signed the papers, he walks home, each turn in the path a private goodbye. Outside their hut Grace is preparing their evening meal: steamed cassava, sweet potatoes, kidney beans. Soon, he thinks, soon she will be able to have chicken also. Inside he drags out the box, unlocking it with the key tied on a string under his shirt. Carefully he counts: the agency man requires 1200 shillings for travel, 600 for uniform, 250 commission. He thinks of the very fine room, the very good job, a salary.

All around him are the sounds of evening: wives cooking, children playing, insects buzzing. He hears the rhythmic slap, stamp, slap as Iminza skips, the frayed rope-ends twisted around her palms. Mbone throws small stones towards a series of circles scratched in the dust and Saliku, squatting beside them, squeals each time one reaches the target. Mmberane thinks of marbles, of a sturdy, rainbow-coloured rope.

And, for a moment only, of stifling heat, canned music, hooting horns. There is a pain beneath his breastbone, but he thrusts it away.

The agency man has said the matatu will leave at eight. Mmberane knows it will not; still he will not risk being late. He thinks of the hotel in Mombasa where he will open doors and carry cases, of the fat tips from wealthy tourists, of his first wage. He thinks of the cloth for Grace. He thinks of later, when he has saved enough to bring his family to the fine house: where Grace will cook indoors, where their mattress will not be stuffed with rags. He thinks of school for all his children and of the beach where he will watch them play, curling their toes around the warm sand.

He refuses to think of the stories he has heard.

Poem by *Robert Leach*

Fragments : India

1. Malabar
Bee-eater on a branch
The boatman's steady straining at his punt pole
Poet breathing

2. Coromandel
Balaji quite forgot
His promise to come to the cricket.
He relaxed on his swing
Under lush greenery, while
Sehwag and Tendulkar
Flourished.

3. Chowringhee
Mr Jog, from the specs up, works
Kinetic graphs, account ledgers, financial charts;
Below
Is his heart.

4. Hazrat Nizamuddin
Past the dolphin-shouldering shoals
Of hustling pilgrims, grimy hucksters
Pouring round the Sufi saint's sufficient golden shrine –
A courtyard with
Half a dozen lads at cricket,
A furtive mongoose,
And Ghalib the poet
In his stone place.

5. Indus

Aeon-ancient Hind-cradle
Draped among mountains,
As if
Dropped yesterday.

6. Shantiniketin

Hoopoe
On a half-built, rose-pink wall,
Unfazed by
The busy, drilling building site.

7. Ghar Par

Seeing my picture in a theatre programme
Long after,
I remembered
The green fans of the coconut palms
In Mamallapuram.

'In Hindi **'Asha'** means 'hope'. **'Ghar Par'** means 'at home'.

Paintings by Joy Parker: Page 12 - Boatman; page 13 - Asha'

Non Fiction by *Lynne Henderson*

Coming Home

'You're in the middle of nowhere, here like!' said the strapping Geordie delivery lad, throwing me a grin as he handed down a box from the lorry to his mate. He'd just driven down a two and a half mile single track road of peaks and troughs, through a patchwork quilt of fields with the slumbering backbone of the Eildon Hills on the far horizon.

I beamed back at him, held in the gaze of a spring sunshine. It was music to my ears, just what I'd intended. It was the dream come true. A country cottage in the middle of nowhere. Of course, it's not really so isolated. But if you consider that we all too easily get snowed in, that we can hand our outgoing letters to the postie, that we're six miles from the nearest shop – then that will do for me. And of course it's relative to where you've come from.

Born and bred in Durham City, I'd been living with my husband in Winchcombe, Gloucestershire, in a suburban modern bungalow, the house we bought when we got married. Life in the Cotswolds was good for seven years or so with convenient employment in the nearby promenade spa town of Cheltenham. We were northern England folk in the deep south and we had plenty to discover.

In our spare time we toured the Cotswold towns and villages where staddle stone mushrooms budded in the winding lanes; where fat ginger cats lazed on top of garden walls and on bone china mugs; where licks of ice-cream melted in tourists' hands, where ducks preened and posed for photographs on the banks of slow sliding waters snaking under low arches. Where in the cool of medieval churches lay knights and their ladies in stately rest, close to their country manors and box hedge gardens. Still preserved for posterity the mullion stones, the leaded panes, the oak slab doors. This is how I like to remember it – the highlights.

So why was it I bought a big print of an oil painting entitled 'Border Country' showing a collie on a misted hillside by a loch and hung it above the fireplace? Why was it my husband and I started going on holiday to the Western Isles, where a work colleague back in Cheltenham said 'there's nothing there though'. And ultimately why was it we decided we wanted to move here to the Borders? 'You're moving to Scotland?' my boss said to me, looking puzzled. 'Why there? It's cold and it rains all the time.'

Well there are many reasons why; they shift and surge like the pull of the tide.

There are those early family holidays, those tours my parents insisted upon when my sister and I were teenagers. My father loved taking to the open road and his favourite trips were into Scotland which meant we always headed north from Durham to Carter Bar. As the green Ford twisted, turned and climbed its way to the top of the world, past open hills stippled with brush tufts of rush and reed, and crowned with stands of firs and pines, we entered an open country, a wilderness. We were pioneers of a kind, rolling along in our covered wagon. I still feel this mounting excitement ascending Carter Bar when I drive back across the Border after a family visit. But back then my sister and I were compelled to take our cue as soon as Dad pointed out the road sign telling us 'Welcome to Scotland'. 'Wow,' we'd chant – and the seeds were sewn.

We had a Scottish surname too. There weren't very many Hendersons in Durham or in the Cotswolds. I kept hold of it after I got married. My dad discovered the Henderson clan had been the personal bodyguard of the chief of the clan MacDonald of Glencoe. Their motto was 'Virtue Alone Ennobles'. Later on I found Dad a whiskey tumbler with these words engraved on it - not words to forge a fighting charge through moorland heather into battle, but a quiet truth to try to live by. It's also true to say that there have been plenty of Hendersons in the Borders throughout the centuries, so when we drove up from Durham, in a way we were coming home.

We would trek on up into the majestic Highlands, going west, passing glassy lochs, through craggy glens, through barren terrain, to take a ferry over to Skye and to the Outer Hebrides. Rocky roads and passing places were unchartered territory, to make real that adventuring dream. But always we came back through the Borderlands. I still have a small souvenoir jug showing forget-me-nots on a creamy ground, with the town of Hawick printed upon it. I never knew then how to pronounce Hawick: How–wick I would have said then. And it never was forgotten.

Another big pull to the Borders has to be the its rich and varied landscape. Of course in the Cotswolds I suppose I couldn't complain. There were plenty of fields, farms, walking tracks and rights of way. But somehow it just never felt right, something was always missing. It was too soft: the grass grew too tall, the hedges too high, the trees too shrubby and scrubby, the land not marked out enough. There were no bristling rushes in boggy ground, the hills had been modelled by moles and the sheep didn't nibble hard enough to kept the fields mowed. There were no giant hogweed umbrellas crowding the banks of streams. There was no open road, no moorland, no 'in the middle of nowhere' space for me. So after a couple of holidays in the Borders, driving up from the South, the Border Country pulled me back and we settled here. It became home.

Like my father, I like the open road. And every time I drive through the Borders from the middle of nowhere to somewhere, I relish what I see - my favourite features, moving through the seasons.

There are the changing textures of farmers fields, from the deeply etched furrows to take the seed, to the slow flush of saffron as the oil seed rape matures, to the breathing of the wind over barley fields, to the stark stubble of harvest time.

There's the circling glide of a buzzard in the blue, its keen eye seeking prey in twitching blades of green.

There's the rosebay willow herb and its blushes of pink in summer with its whiplashed cotton wool seed heads in a hoar-frosted hedgerow.

There are the Eildons low-lying in the distance as a reassuring presence when I tramp the fields, when a pheasant is frightened into a flurried frenzy of wings.

I love the conifer plantations cresting the swells of the land like ocean surf. Then closer, they stand on high ground, like grouped battalions, feathery spears pointed to the sky and ready to command. Even softened in winter by powder sprinkles of snow crystals, they still silently wait for the call.

I love the border hedges, unruly hawthorn sculpted by farmers into silhouetted fans. Streamline trimmed they stride the border edges and mark out contours in the land.

I love the arc of silver in an early dawn as a leaping salmon rides the Tweed.

These are the essences of where I call home.

Parrot in Darnick

Your loud cry got interest from the kestrel
and me I waded nettles and hawthorn looking
for its fledgling straight through your green
until you followed me back from school
to shout obscenities from the leylandii
that I would have cut down yesterday
they are my neighbours' pets.

I showed you a banana and an orange
pulled from deep down my magician's sleeve
your big beak gutting a plum
nothing left but a flap of purpled skin
you disappeared goaded by crows:
what on earth were you doing here again?
And why didn't I go with you?

Poem by *Bridget Khursheed*

The Last Dance

Fiction by *Oliver Eade*

A Spanish son-in-law and a Spanish daughter-in-law.

Coincidence? Yes, although son and daughter each found his/her Hispanic life partner via the Scottish educational system. Son and daughter-in-law were post-graduate students together in the same department at Edinburgh University; our daughter, via Aberdeen University, and whilst studying Spanish in Granada, met her future intended when working in a bar (an 'educational experience', mind you). The Borders link? Excellent local state schools that ensured our offspring places in Scottish universities ...launching pads for taking off into that world beyond the Borders.

So now I can leave the Borders behind and concentrate not just on 'Spain' but the Spanish 'alma' or 'soul'. We hear a lot about the atrocities inflicted on China by Chairman Mao (my wife is Chinese) but little is said about the horrors of the Franco period in Spain. It's almost as if Spain is trying to forget her shame by hiding it in dark corners, but it's there... gnawing at the souls of those who suffered...like Carmen, Pablo and Pedro...

Carmen Ruiz glances at her watch for the hundredth time. Forty-five minutes late! That might be within the bounds of punctuality for most Spanish men, but not Pedro. He's never late. Something must be wrong. An accident? No! Impossible! Pedro's the safest driver in Andalucia. How she loves to be driven home by him for she knows no harm could come to her with Pedro at the wheel.

And she feels safe in his arms when they dance. Life became uncertain and hollow, all those years living alone. Often, she got a feeling that something terrifying and Franco-shaped might leap at her from the hollowness and destroy her, but after befriending Pedro at the salon de baile one Saturday evening, the hollowness and the fear left her. Now life has a purpose: to dance. They say true dancing partnerships are born out of a yearning of two souls to move together as one, not a forcing together of separate beings who act in opposition on the dance floor. So it is with Carmen and Pedro. They danced as one all that first evening...and the week after and the week after that.

Pedro, inordinately shy off the dance floor, is an organic farmer. One week he brought a bag full of organic vegetables for Carmen as she'd owned up to being an excellent cook. He handed her the vegetables with a nod and almost a smile, but when she told him she couldn't possibly carry the bag home on the bus, for her back would give her hell if she tried, his face lit up. His expression told her everything. The vegetable offering was his way of telling her their relationship should shift upwards a notch or two; her response: a request that he drive her home that evening. Thereafter he drove her home every week, and she would always invite him in for a little tapas and a glass of Malaga.

The conversation was only ever one way. Pedro would sit, keeping a respectful distance and listening intently to Carmen's life history delivered in widow-sized instalments. Some evenings he'd be sitting there for two or more hours, but he'd not change his position and one glass of wine was his limit. He'd never been drunk in all his sixty-eight years and was proud of the fact.

Carmen's husband, Pablo, died from alcohol poisoning of the liver some ten years back. Their last fifteen years as husband and wife were spent living apart in the same house, Pablo upstairs and Carmen downstairs. It was the only way she could tolerate him and they communicated through their son in Seville, eighty kilometres away. Occasionally, they would pass each other in the entrance hall as one came in and the other went out, but not a word would be exchanged.

And Pablo never danced.

Ten years a widow and fifteen years in the same house as Pablo...that's twenty-five years of loneliness to make up with Pedro and she has savoured every second of their time together, especially on the dance floor. There's no dance they haven't been able to master: waltz, foxtrot, jive, paso doble, quickstep - anything - and he once told her it's truly remarkable she never danced before and that she must be a natural. His shyness melts away when he holds her close, but she often wonders how many other women he's held like that, for one thing is certain: he was an expert dancer long before they first tripped the light fantastic together.

Curiously, she has no idea whether he's a bachelor or a widower. She's never asked and he's never said. She only knows he lives by himself, like her, and that he must be very wealthy judging by the extent of his lands.

She began cooking for him. The tapas was just the starter to tempt him. He now loves her pollo and her patatas a la pobre and her cakes. He turns up mid-afternoon, every Saturday, and they eat together, no wine, as she spills out her heart, offloading some of the pain of the Franco period, and then he drives her to the dance hall and they dance and dance and dance and he drives her home and she gives him more tapas and a glass of Malaga and they talk until the early hours...when he finally leaves and she holds onto the memory of him and, once asleep, dreams again of dancing.

Perhaps if Pablo had danced things would have turned out differently. Unlike Pedro, the man jabbered incessantly and drank. At first, as a young woman, she felt sorry for him. A child in Franco's dark and sorrowful Spain, all opportunities for success were denied him because his family happened to be on the wrong side of the divide. He was skilful with his hands and should have been a cabinet maker, like his father before Franco's thugs killed him, but the authorities saw to it Pablo got nowhere in his career. He ended up a labourer on the roads; a labourer who could recite Lorca, who crafted small animals for children out of bits of old wood, and probably she did love him then, perhaps to mother him and maybe turn him into what he should have been, but gradually, as their son grew up and diverted that love away from her husband, the alcohol thing progressed from habit to addiction. Initially it was shame that caused her to banish the drunken Pablo upstairs; shame that she'd failed him in some way and that the neighbours would blame her for the rows. But the shame turned to disgust and the disgust remained with her till Pablo's death, his body rotted by alcohol.

At seventy-two years of age she should know happiness is an illusion; that it doesn't last and that loneliness always returns, its bleakness reinforced by brief interludes of illusion.

At the very least she should have read the warning signs last week when they danced their last dance together. It was a waltz. Pedro kept looking over her right shoulder, steering her purposively around other gliding couples to keep a certain person within his sights: an elegant, dyed brunette, not a day over sixty, with legs that could have belonged to a woman half her age. Carmen did notice the shy exchange of smiles between them after that dance; she tried to persuade herself they were already acquainted and that these were no more than smiles of recognition, and she promised him her special pollo today. It should have been so obvious when he phoned this afternoon to say he's too busy for the meal and will collect her on the way to the salon de baile, but her mind refused to accept the pain of deceit. She'd had enough of that in the past...enough of pain.

But an hour has passed and she can no longer deny the pain. She returns her dance shoes to their box in her shoe cupboard, slips out of her dance dress, hangs it at the far end of her wardrobe, never to be worn again, and prepares for herself some tapas. Perhaps, she thinks, she should allow herself two glasses of Malaga this time to soften that pain. Then she can pray; pray, with those fading embers of hope fanned by Malaga that one day the other woman's legs will grow old and he will realise what a rare and wonderful thing a true dancing partnership can be.

Names changed, Carmen, Pablo and Pedro are known to my daughter. And the Spanish soul? It'll always live on...through dance.

Cycling the Border Line

Poem by Fiona Hunt

Inspired by projects in the Tweed Valley, Scottish Borders to convert
disused railway lines into multi-user trails. With thanks and apologies to
WH Auden for 'Night Mail'

This is the bike-trail crossing the Borders,
Bringing two-wheeled fathers and daughters.
Cycling from the East, cycling from the West
Who can tell which way is best?

Cruising through Peebles, alongside the Tweed,
Coffee and cakes: that's what we need!
Through the deep tunnel, and out into light
Across the viaduct at a tremendous height.

Looking down on the tumbling waters,
We pause to chat with friendly walkers.
Cattle raise their heads as we sail past,
Serene in the meadows, richly grassed.

We'll cycle in rain but prefer the sun,
A wind on our backs makes it much more fun.
Some pedal fast and work up a sweat,
Others go slow with friends they have met.

Cyclists from the South, cyclists from the North,
They head this way from over the Forth.
Thin tyres, thick tyres, mudguards or no.
'Horse-rider in front, remember - go slow!'

Bikes with two wheels, or maybe with three,
Some with a trailer for the very wee.
Bikes that are blue, red, white or black,
All will be welcome to use this track.

Who are the Scots?

Non fiction by *Pat Mosel*

Muscular. Granular. Stone-faced statue standing on a hillside in a sparse winter wood, overlooking Dryburgh Abbey, out of the way of cities and present battlefields and parliaments, in the countryside of the Scottish Borders. Mighty. Maybe fifteen foot high. This is the legend of William Wallace, Commander in the Scottish Wars of Independence eight centuries ago; hanged, drawn and quartered on 23 August 1305. Best known today as Braveheart, the hero of the film starring Mel Gibson that inspired patriotic feelings in many, including those who knew nothing of Scotland. What would Wallace think of the Scotland of today, with its intended referendum to test opinion on independence from England?

Stone. He knows nothing of this development. Or, does he?

He fought. He believed. Guerrilla leader, an outlaw, a legend some say. He beheaded; he burned castles. The Gurardian of Scotland, he amassed troops. He hated the English, initially for killing his father. He protested. He suffered. No hint of parliamentarians in slick suits. His world was mud and guts and blood, vomit and stench. He died but his cause is not dead. The suits and ties and fashion wear are now the armour. Alex Salmond, First Minister of a devolved Scotland is likely to lead Scotland to independence, if it happens. But who are the Scots? Is there a description that defines a Scot?

This statue of William Wallace is tucked away on a Borders hillside for a reason. It is because Scots nationalism has been buried and festering for a long time. It has been aggressively hidden from the tourists, from the foreigners, in part from the English. Yet now, a substantial proportion of the English are said to be in favour of Scottish independence. Not the Coalition British Prime Minister, David Cameron. He was in Scotland in February 2012 to give and emotive speech on the advantages of union. He said England, Scotland, Wales and Northern Ireland are much stronger as the United Kingdom but he did not deal with the details, like what would happen to Benefits for the Disabled, said Salmond, adding that Scottish independence is about people and not about prestige. The two men are closer to an agreement on how the referendum will be phrased, when it happens.

Wallace was a warrior Scot. How deep is his legacy? Will 'Braveheart' be screened just before the Referendum? Two tourists join us at his feet, with mud on their boots. A light breeze stirs in the woods; a spirit, a ghost, a wind. These two tourists, a man and a young girl, speak in French. The Scots have long been friends with the French, although Wallace fell out with them at times. The tourists don't linger. They have come for a walk rather than to pay homage. They move on down the path that gets muddier and muddier, like the complex question of independence. If Scotland becomes independent, families will be split up. Scots live all over the world but they also live in England and the English live in Scotland. The present Prime Minister of Britain, the UK, is English but the last two Prime Ministers, Gordon Brown and Tony Blair came from Scotland. How is that for integration!

One of the most remarkable things about William Wallace is that fully grown he was six foot seven inches in height in the thirteenth century, a giant and of great stature as this statue shows. Large hands that slew countless men. Huge thighs and calves, and feet that served him on the run when he hid out in forests. Most men at that time would have been five foot or smaller. And it was a time when battle raged and brawn counted. The English killed his wife - they had to be repaid.

About the time of Wallace's birth Edward 1 came to the throne of England and he was the one - after the Wars of Independence and other battles and skirmishes - who saw to it that Walllace, after a farce of a trial, was publicly humiliated and done to death in a brutal fashion. Wallace's cause was never helped by the divisions amongst the nobles in Scotland itself. He, himself, was the son of a minor nobleman.

Sir William Wallace, at one time Guardian of Scotland, hid out in the woods and forests just as he is hiding in this wood, a giant statue in the Scottish Borders. So, here I stand in front of a hero; an outlaw when English were colonising Scotland, a leader to victory, a diplomat; Braveheart.

It is easy to stand in front of this statue and marvel that not a finger moves, not a hand lifts a sword, not a muscle stretches, not an eyelid flickers. Stone. Granular. Composed.

I am not a Scot, although my maternal grandmother was and I have lived in Scotland for over thirty years. As yet, I have no idea how I will vote in a referendum. Born in what was then "Southern Rhodesia", I have my own history of knowing suppression and bloodshed. And the fight goes on.

Every time I meet new people in the UK and they hear my muted accent they presume I am South African. If they are old enough, you can see their minds speeding to Apartheid and the great Nelson Mandela. When I say no, I am Zimbabwean (reluctantly, because I don't like what Robert Mugabe is doing to the country), if they are old enough, their minds speed to Ian Smith, majority rule, guerrillas or terrorists and Independence. I can't persuade them that my parents were among the two percent of White Rhodesians who never voted for Ian Smith and UDI. Or worse still, the conservative minded say, 'Ian Smith, jolly good chap.'

Sometimes I feel like a statue, just standing here on God's earth looking at the beautiful hills beyond while people debate the politics of my background.'

The joke is that my friends and I, who are now sixty plus, were effectively brought up in the nineteenth century. One thing is for sure, I was taught to believe in Great Britain as the Motherland and 2012 is Queen Elizabeth 11's Diamond Jubilee year. Cheers!

And we have a new princess.

Ah! You thought you'd guessed my vote. But you haven't. It's far more likely to be based on the state of the UK economy as a whole at the time.

William Wallace statue stand.

Fiction by *Tom Bryan*

Dr Jaybird

Pervert? Molester? Thief? Genius? Poor Old Soul? A miser, rich in shiny gold? Doctor Jaybird, tall. dressed in blue wool, sailor's cap, shaggy grey hair and one blue eye patch over his right eye. Terrifies the neighbourhood children as he marches down the alley, the border of our unfenced back-yards. He comes by at the same time every morning, about ten o'clock, looks neither left nor right, parades down the alley and out of sight.

Post-war Canadian housing estate, the soldiers came home and started families in these pastel bungalows, unfenced yards where the children were spilled outside in all weathers by their house-proud mothers. This meant Jaybird always had a full audience for his parade, a multi-lingual one at that. Our street: Ukrainian, Polish, British, Norwegian, Quebecois.

Skip rope,
'Fudge, fudge, call the judge, momma's got a newborn baa-by,
wrap him up in tissue paper send him down the elevator….'
Tag *'You're it….'* Hush. A speck to the left increasing in size, silhouette looming larger, children sheltering away from the alley, then the silhouette receding, vanishing.

Dr Jaybird? The name?
'Coz he hoards shiny things, just like a bluejay.'
'Naw, he dresses in blue, black and white, just like a jaybird.'
'Where he stays, in the shack at the end of the alley, there's jaybirds every-where.'

Occupation (according to adults)
He was a doctor once but had a nervous breakdown after accidentally killing a patient and started living like a hermit and tramp, on his war pension.
Poor old soul. Was shell-shocked in the war and lives alone, drawing his pension.
He's well spoken, a scholar, who speaks several languages.
Collects old metal, trash can stuff, sells it for enough money to buy food.
Alkie. Sits in his shack drinking all night.
Paedophile, been in and out of prison. The police know about him, keep an eye on him. I told my kids to never go near him and to never go to the end of the alley.
Spring. He's muffled, lean from hibernation, blue collar up against the dark tumbling prairie sky (the children whisper down the alley, *here he is again, survived another winter in his shack*)
Summer. Blue sky against our emerald yards, he appears, jacket open, blue shirt underneath, and his walk is a summer saunter, dawdling.

Autumn. Coat buttoned up, he's stooped to the wind, geese overhead. 'Geese are the dead souls of men,' said Mary Churchenko who knew about things like that.

Winter. Hooded sweatshirt over the blue jacket, face deep and hidden. Some whispering. *He kills children in winter, that's when he's at his worst.* And in winter we flood our back yards with hoses from kitchen taps. We skate and skate in the great ice rink of the yards, warmed by our parkas from Eaton's and the Hudson Bay Company. We are green, red and pink on the frozen ice and our houses are the same colour, waiting for the colours of Spring but Dr. Jaybird does not often go afield in winter until he returns like the geese.

A few said they had no fear of a crazy bearded man, an old coot, a phoney sailor.

But.

But we never saw him return down our alley from the other direction, ever.

'Comes back late at night when we're all indoors.'

'Comes back down another street or alley, not down ours.'

'Comes back early in the morning, before we get up.'

Child words. *Killer. Murderer. Gold. Miser. Vampire. Wolfman.*

Adult words. *Pension. Welfare. Shell shock.*

Nobody had ever seen Jaybird take anything from trash cans, in fact we had never seen him carry anything at all.

Then one day my prize walleye pike went missing. This walleye fish was a beauty. Nearly 18 inches, weighed two pounds, I'd caught him on a red and white spinner, from a local pond. He ran deep, then jumped a few times but I'd reeled him in. My grandfather put the walleye still flopping in a live bait bucket and the fish survived the drive home. I put him in rain barrel at the side of the house, covered with a screen weighted down with a brick. We threw earthworms in from time to time and every day he was a familiar moving shadow in the barrel bottom.

I sensed an odd connection between the old man and the fish, both survivors, both there every day. One June morning I went to the barrel. The screen and brick were in place but the barrel was empty, no shadow, and no fish. A few minutes, along the parade route, we gathered for Dr. Jaybird but for the first time that summer, he never came. It broke up our summer routine, but he was not there the next day or the day after that. Nor did my fish re-appear in the barrel. Larry Broad had the idea.

'Someone saw crazy Jaybird with a big fish sticking out his pocket. The other day. I bet it was your fish. Had to be. He'll have eaten it by now.'

Had to be. That old bastard. Thief. That crazy old man took my fish but I would get it back. To get to our rain barrel he would have to walk across the whole back yard, between two houses, practically under our windows. We would easily have seen him and there were plenty neighbourhood dogs to bark warning. I had secret doubts that the old man took the fish but I was angry, angry enough to take my bait bucket and head down the alley, towards where I believed old Jaybird lived. Aged 12, on my own, I would confront Dr. Jaybird and get my fish back! Simple.

It was a bright day and I was up ahead of everybody. I walked further than the last gardens I had ever been to, past Andrewchuk, Nystrom, Douglas, Wulwand. I finally came to where the alley branched as a T-junction, leading to parallel streets. A fence bounded the end of the alley. A wooden stile crossed the fence. The field where I had to cross was full of thistles and scraggy willows. The path faded into the distance, into a clump of cottonwood trees. The sun had gone behind a cloud; it had become grey and chill. I left the path, hid behind some cottonwoods, and waited. The old man would normally have left his shack (not yet visible) at about 9:30 in order to pass our house at about 10 a.m. I waited from 9 a.m. Fifteen minutes, twenty minutes, half an hour. I crept further along the path until I could see the shack--- an old garden shed, unpainted, one visible window to the right of the door. Slowly, heart thumping, I crept beneath the window, and taking a deep breath, stood up high enough to peer in the window. I couldn't see any evidence of my fish anywhere.

The police came later, when I ran home and told everybody what I saw. The shack was dark inside and at first, I couldn't see anything clearly. When I opened the door, two rats ran over my shoes. Dr. Jaybird was slumped dead over a dingy card table, his eyes open and staring. Around the shack, glinting on every surface and every space, hung mobiles and chimes made of shining objects: marbles, tin cans, old fishing lures, shards of broken glass, just like the broken beer bottle in his own left hand that must have cut the veins in his right wrist. Bleeding deltas ran over the green felt table. The blood glistened in the rays of the morning sun.

Outside, jaybirds heckled from the willows, their blue and white feathers ruffled by the rising breeze, their bright eyes shining like baubles.

East, West

Poem by *Pim Claridge*

in the hurly-burly-hubbub of his hot Malaysian town,
where the heat is sapping energy from city-weary souls
it's too hot, and too humid, and too crowded and too busy
as the battered tins of beggars slowly fill.

the trees are laced with lights and Chinese-chatter-babble rises
as the evening call to prayer flutters, fluting-high, and sweet
above the hurly-burly-hubbub of that hot Malaysian town!
while here in the maelstrom of frantic Christmas shopping
overheated, overladen shoppers push and shove and spend
until they are exhausted and just longing to go home,
and the caps lying on the pavement slowly fill.

outside it is freezing and breath freezes in my throat
and then I see the castle, black against the star-laced sky
and wonder, if he remembers, how it used to be,
in these old streets so familiar, our home, and me?
memories came flooding, and suddenly I'm warm, and comforted
in this historic, grand and beautiful, but freezing Scottish town!

Published in Shadow on the Sand, see www.pimclaridge.com for further information.

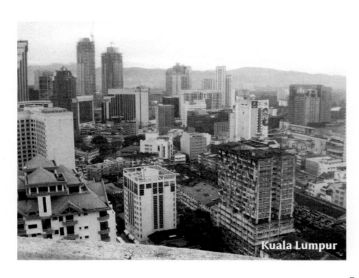

Kuala Lumpur

DOMESTIC MEDICINE,

Or, A TREATISE on the

PREVENTION AND CURE

of DISEASES, by

REGIMEN AND SIMPLE MEDICINES:

With Obfervations concerning

SEA-BATHING,

And on the Ufe of

THE MINERAL WATERS.

TO WHICH IS ANNEXED,

A DISPENSATORY FOR THE USE OF PRIVATE PRACTITIONERS.

By WILLIAM BUCHAN, M.D.

FELLOW OF THE ROYAL COLLEGE OF PHYSICIANS, EDINBURGH.

The Twenty=firft Edition,

With confiderable Additions, and various Notes;

By A. P. BUCHAN, M.D.

OF THE ROYAL COLLEGE OF PHYSICIANS, LONDON;

AND

PHYSICIAN TO THE WESTMINSTER HOSPITAL.

LONDON:

PRINTED FOR T. CADELL AND W. DAVIES; F. C. AND J. RIVINGTON; J. WALKER; J. CUTHELL; WILKIE AND ROBINSON; DARTON AND HARVEY; LACKINGTON, ALLEN, AND CO.; LONGMAN, HURST, REES, ORME, AND BROWN; JOHN RICHARDSON; J. M. RICHARDSON; C. LAW; B. AND R. CROSBY; J. LLOYD; SHERWOOD, NEELY, AND JONES; AND J. JOHNSON AND CO.; AND FOR W. CREECH, AT EDINBURGH.

1813.

William Buchan, M.D. – How the man from the Borders and his medicine bestrode the world.

Non Fiction by *Gwen Chessell*

Dr William Buchan is largely forgotten now but during his lifetime in the late 18th century and into the early 19th, his influence on the health and well-being of families all over Britain, in America and in some of the colonies, was profound and would last for almost two centuries. It would lead to his being accorded a place of burial in the pantheon of the British great and good. It brought his surviving son and daughter and many other mourners through the grassy Abbey garth of Westminster Abbey on the morning of 6 March 1805 to the hushed and shaded west cloisters. They had come to honour the passing and interment of a man who had been a friend to many and a source of relief and edification to countless families who never knew him personally. William Buchan, whose coffin was being laid to rest in a place that held the remains of those who had made an impact on the life of the country, kings and commoners alike, their final resting place chosen according to their degree in life, was far from his beginnings in 1729 in the small Border village of Ancrum. It was perhaps fitting that the west cloisters had been chosen to receive the body of a man so steeped in the art of instructing others because it was here that the novices of the Abbey monastery were taught by the novice master in the days before Henry VIII placed his avaricious hands on religious establishments.

William Buchan's father held a small estate in the Ancrum area and from an early age, his son displayed a talent for healing. Perhaps family pressure led him in a different direction initially, for it was to study Divinity that William entered Edinburgh University. By March 1755, he had had a change of heart and enrolled to study Medicine and was fortunate to do so under Professor John Gregory, the man who coined the word 'patient' to describe those who were known then simply as 'the sick'.

On graduation in 1758, Buchan's career led him on the path that was to take him away from Scotland and lead to his life's work. While in Edinburgh, he had married and on graduating, moved with his wife to Yorkshire. What prompted the move is not known – why does anyone leave their birthplace and their kith and kin and the settled environment where all is known and usually loved. So many Scots moved away from their roots then; some by choice and motivated purely by ambition, some by circumstances beyond their control or by economic necessity but for whatever reason, educated Scots were welcome in all spheres of thought and occupation. Scotland in 1758 was a power-house of enlightenment and learning and it almost seems as if the country was too small to hold all those questing, inspirational minds. Her universities produced thinkers of influence and renown and the momentum of the Scottish Enlightenment was to propel Scottish intellectualism forward into the developing technological world. It would leave a lasting and indelible impression on the centuries to come.

William Buchan was part of this and it may have been what happened while he was in Yorkshire that led him to posterity. Here he undertook the medical care of children in an orphanage in Ackworth with a salary of £42 a year, a stipend that excluded his board and his horse. Nothing is known of his wife other than her surname of Peter but the Westminster Abbey Burial Lists record that she had pre-deceased her husband and that it was in Ackworth that the Buchans' infant son had died. This may have been the catalyst for what followed in his career. The orphanage closed for lack of government funding. No surprises there - it seems that money was as tight then as it is now, and William Buchan returned to Edinburgh and in 1761 wrote his thesis on the subject that had touched his soul - the preservation of infant life. Some people struck by a tragedy such as the loss of an infant have the courage following such a dreadful event to lead them to do something positive to help others. So it might have been with Dr William Buchan. It may have been the death of his longed-for firstborn that led him to produce, not just his doctoral thesis *De Infantum Vita Conservanda* (On the preservation of infant life), but his monumental self-help work *Domestic Medicine or the Family Physician*. As he said himself, he wished 'to be the happy instrument of alleviating the miseries of those suffering innocents, or of rescuing them from an untimely grave'. William Buchan would end his days furth of the Borders to become the Dr Spock of his day. His book, however, would travel much further afield from the place where it was conceived and earn its creator justifiable plaudits and appreciation.

The first edition appeared in 1769 and was priced expensively at six shillings, a large sum at that time. It was an immediate best seller, despite some adverse comments from those whom the worthy doctor described as his adversaries, medics like himself who felt that he was betraying the mystique and exclusiveness of their profession. This bothered Buchan not a bit - indeed he felt that the adverse publicity given to his book helped its sales considerably. It is a book full of no nonsense, common-sense advice, written to be accessible to the layman. Great emphasis is placed on diet, temperance and hygiene and much of his advice is ahead of its time. It is extremely readable and very interesting. He had no time for old wives' tales and quackery and he was also against medical oligarchy and considered that everyone had a right to know and practise simple healing techniques. To be sure it was not the first book of its kind but its predecessors *Le Médecin des Pauvres* (Medicine for the Poor) by Paul Dubé in 1669 and *Avis au peuple sur la santé* (Advice to people with Respect to their Health) by Samuel Tissot in 1761 failed to have the same acceptance and never really took off. But such advice was clearly needed and even John Wesley had a crack at producing something to help those who could not afford medical help. Some of Wesley's advice in his book *Primitive Physick* should not be tried at home however. He advocated toasted cheese to stop the bleeding in a deep cut. Buchan's book was different and so useful that it was still being used in some remote areas of Scotland in the 1920s, and who knows how many precious copies were carried by the many emigrants who left Scotland to seek better lives in newer worlds.

By 1783, Buchan had dedicated the successive editions to Sir Joseph Banks, the president of the Royal Society and erstwhile naturalist with Captain James Cook when he discovered Australia. By the end of William Buchan's life in 1805 some 80,000 copies, in nineteen editions, had been sold. There was an American edition in 1774, and copies even penetrated the far-off reaches of the Russian empire from where the Empress Catherine the Great honoured him with a gold medal and a letter of appreciation.

By 1778, Buchan's standing in the medical world enabled him to carry on a thriving practice in London, where patients flocked to see him in the Chapter Coffee House near St Paul's Cathedral. By 1804, his health had broken down and he died early in 1805. His work was carried on by his son, Alexander Peter Buchan, also a doctor, who saw to it that *Domestic Medicine* was kept up to date and marched with the times. My own edition dates from 1813 and contains additional information inserted by Dr Alexander Buchan who himself wrote medical books and who was also interred in due course in the cloisters in Westminster Abbey. William Buchan would have been proud of him too.

The Lion and the Unicorn
An old story for modern times

Elizabeth of England was dead and left no children to climb upon her throne. When she died her coat of arms had a shield with supporters of a golden lion on the most important dexter side (left viewed from the front) and a red dragon on the sinister side. A successor was sought after her death and in 1603 it was decided that James VI of Scotland would become James the 1st of England and so be monarch of both nations.

Scottish Coat of Arms, Melrose Abbey

The Scottish coat of arms has two white unicorns supporting a shield. James merged both coats of arms and being first a Scot, gave the unicorn the important side and the lion the lesser side. He spent most of his time in England and told the Parliament there that he ruled Scotland by his pen.

Union of the Crowns, Galashiels post office

When his son, Charles I inherited the kingdoms he let the lion chase the unicorn to the lesser side of the shield to make his English coat of arms.

After over 100 years, the parliaments of these two great nations decided to unite. The Monarchs had been based mainly in England at this time, and in 1707 when the parliaments amalgamated and a British coat of arms became such that the golden lion took pride of place and the unicorn followed at the other side.

The Golden Lion represents power and strength and the White Unicorn symbolises peace and tranquillity. The Golden Lion also stands for the golden sun while the White Unicorn is the pale moon.

Legend has it that the lion will forever chase the unicorn but will never catch it. But if ever it should, then the moon will always overshadow the sun. Never the other way.

Old English nursery rhyme
The lion and the unicorn were fighting for the crown
The lion beat the unicorn all around the town
Some gave them white bread and some gave them brown
Some gave them plum cake and ran them out of town

Union of the Parliaments and current, Berwick barracks

Hizzy's Honour

Poem by *Christopher Ryan*

the good of the day
came in the slow thunder drive-by
of a thousand bikers
brandished leather on rolling chrome
metallic red and blue and black rubber
the crowds stopped shopping
stood waved and welcomed him home

Hizzy died the accidental death of heroes
he fell out of the sky
upon Carlenrig field
41 years old God bless him
and now they honour him
canonised in cold bronze
set in stone

do we know the gift we receive
in honouring a single man?
the happiness death brings
after the tears?
in the memories of glory
in cheers and smiles
and the grand excuse to drive for hours
a hundred miles or more together
and a thousand engines roar
to honour one man
among the flowers
beneath the trees
beside the river

I mean to say -
how wonderful it is
we honour ourselves
when we honour a single one of us
who mirrors our dreams
riding glory beyond death

The Leet Water

The Anthology theme, 'Scottish Borders and Beyond' suggests an outflow of people and things—enforced or voluntary emigration during the 19th century onwards and the export of raw materials and finished goods. Border people have also exported or taken with them, their ideas, art and skills; the literature of the Scottish Borders comes particularly to mind with the works of Buchan, Hogg, Scott and so many others, that have achieved worldwide recognition.

However, my sights were set quite differently because, looking at the map, my attention was drawn to the many spidery tendrils, the intense network of watercourses, all contributing to the single catchment area of the mighty River Tweed. This suggested a huge outflow, a physical one, millions of gallons of water flowing through the Scottish Borders down to the Scottish Tweed, then along the border into England and out into the North Sea.

I then looked at the smallest part of this system, just one of those tendrils, too small even to be called a river, the course of which although entirely within the Scottish Borders (as it flows into the Tweed at Coldstream) produces a flow of water that goes far beyond. The Leet Water is something over twelve or thirteen miles in length, rising in Whitsome parish, flowing through Swinton parish, along the Eccles parish boundary into Coldstream parish. In 1885, Francis H. Groome, editor of the *Ordnance Gazetteer of Scotland: A Survey of Scottish Topography etc.* described it as having 'a slow and sluggish current'. This is true, except in times of spate, but the lazy flow of a small river or 'water' meandering through pastures and meadows has an appeal all of its own—it must do because the Leet Water has certainly exercised its charms on me.

The derivation of Leet Water may be from the Old English *wætergelæt* meaning 'open watercourse to conduct water'. The Old Northumbrian dialect gives *let* and Middle Scots (the Anglic language of Lowland Scotland used until the late 16th C.) gives *leit*. So, the nearby village of Leitholm may have derived from the Old English *gelætham* meaning 'farm by the water conduit'. Leet Water could have got its name from man-made 'leets', 'leats' or 'lades' extracting channelled water for the mills along its length. However, it is probable that the name precedes these and is more likely to have been derived from the general term for a natural watercourse.

I have said that the Leet is not a river and there is good precedence for this. A sketch map of St. Mary's Abbey, Coldstream, dated 1589 describes the Leet as the 'watter of leet'. Sharpe's map of Coldstream in 1818 describes it merely as 'Leet' and both John Blackadder's map of 1797 and Crawford and Brooke's map of 1843 show it clearly as 'Leet Water'. The designation, 'Water' is probably the term used in the Scottish Borders for all streams smaller than rivers and larger than burns. The term 'stream' is certainly not often found in Scotland but Coldstream is a rare example and it may be that it was originally applied to the Leet Water and then transferred to the settlement beside it.

The Leet Water is often missed off any list of tributaries of the River Tweed because of its undemonstrative size. Other tributaries include the Whiteadder, the Till, the Eden, the Teviot, the Leader, the Gala, the Ettrick, the Leithen, the Quair, the Eddlestone, the Manor, the Lyne and the Holms. However, most of these (exceptions are the Till, [which is mostly in England] and the Teviot) are usually named 'Water' rather than 'River' so, in Lowland Scots terminology, they are distinguishable from the major rivers. The Leet is very unusual in terms of its directional flow in that at no point does it run in the same seaward direction as the River Tweed. Instead it takes an opposite up-river direction, flowing south-west from its source as far as Swintonmill, before swinging south-south west and eventually south-east to meet the Tweed almost at a right-angle, but still longitudinally some one and a quarter miles west of its source in Whitsome parish. This is unlike most tributaries. For example, on the lower Tweed, the River Teviot, the Eden Water and the Whiteadder Water join the River Tweed having conventionally flowed in a seaward direction.

The Leet Water lies entirely within an area of Carboniferous sedimentary rocks termed the 'cement-stone group' because of thin bands of argillaceous (i.e. containing a substantial proportion of clay) limestone often known as 'cement-stone' or 'marl'. The reason for the unusual course of the Leet Water is probably due to the accentuated subglacial landforms of the River Tweed valley particularly to the east of Jedburgh and Kelso. Probably towards the end of the last Ice Age, which ended about 10,000 years ago, the Tweed valley was subject to a glacial 'Palaeo-Ice Stream' (Palaeo from Greek *palaios* meaning ancient). The ice moved downstream caused by sub-glacial melting at ground level due to the pressure of the ice above. The width of the ice-stream was constricted by the Lammermuir Hills to the north and the Cheviot Hills to the south where the ice remained static. The ice-stream narrowed from its 'onset zone' width of about 24 miles south-west of Galashiels to about 12 miles wide in its 'trunk' from Kelso and Coldstream, eastwards.

The movement of the ice-stream caused a change in the land surface beneath the ice. Scouring of the sedimentary Carboniferous sandstones and/or deposition of material in the direction of the ice flow produced many parallel landforms of different sizes, known as 'drumlins' (from Gaelic, *druim* meaning ridge or mound). The height and width of drumlins is greater at the head (the stoss end) and tails off (the lee end) in the

The Leet Water

direction of the ice flow. Drumlins may be 100 to 200 feet high and perhaps up to a mile or so in length and always wider than they are high, but there is great variation depending upon the rate of glacier flow and the type of deposited material.

The Tweed valley has hundreds if not thousands of drumlins and, because all of them lie parallel to the River Tweed, it suggests that they were all laid down by only one ice-stream flowing in the one direction from west to east (or south-west to north-east) within the boundaries of the Tweed valley. The effect of drumlins on the present day landscape is highly visible, for example, on the undulating road between Coldstream and Greenlaw and, very dramatically, on the 'switchback' Duns Road running north from Coldstream. The direction of flow of the Leet Water from its source near Whitsome village would therefore have been affected by the existence of the parallel drumlins that blocked any flow south-eastwards towards the Tweed. A glance at the contours on the Ordnance Survey map (Explorer 346) shows this quite clearly; the fledgling Leet had to find its way south-west instead of south-east and wind its way through lower ground around and between the drumlins before eventually turning south.

The soils along the valleys comprise a rich loam sometimes above a layer of stiff clay or sometimes above gravel. The Leet Water runs through this fertile landscape known as 'The Merse', an area extending from the Lammermuir Hills in the north, to the River Tweed in the south with a breadth from west to east of about twenty miles. The *Blaeu Atlas of Scotland*, 1654 describes the boundaries, history and character of the land and people of the Merse (in Latin) including: '…The whole of the Merse, within the Lammermuir Hills which are blessed with pastures, nourishes with its fertile soil numerous inhabitants, in peace industrious, in war stout-hearted, who used to defend their possessions most bravely against the English…' Before extensive drainage from about 1700 onwards, the land was not all fertile and it may be that the derivation of 'Merse' signifies the original marshy lands or it may relate to the Border areas known as 'Marches'.

The Leet Water is entirely rural, even skirting the built-up areas at Coldstream. It passes through arable land, pasture, woodland, marshland and landed estates. It passes close to country houses, ruined buildings, mill lades and prehistoric and medieval archaeological sites. It has straight sections and 'crinkly' ones, old bridges and new bridges, high cliffs and low embankments. It is a magnet for wildlife and plantlife, a haven for acquatic species and is a valuable spawning ground.

The Leet Water is a delight—it is a gem that deserves to be known beyond the Scottish Borders, but perhaps we would rather keep it a secret.

Poem by *Arthur Parsons*

Venice

An aged beauty full of echoes
The decaying walls, once plastered
By wealth, keep their bent arms-length
And weep stained sorrows to lapping tides

Her youthful exuberance gone
Skin weathered, bones crumbling, embalmed
For voyeurs to gawp the last rites
Of decaying Byzantium

But I have gazed upon her face
She is a witch born of magic
Seeping into unwary hearts
Stealing souls to be her lovers

You can't resist the witch's charms
Ponti and palazzi
Madonnas, masks and mercanti
Enfold you in her rippled arms

As lovers fly to other worlds
The parting leaves a void, an ache
To feel again bemused, bewitched
And taste sea-soaked Venetian mist.

Keep Your Hope Alive

Fiction by *Raghu Shukla*

On a day when Raj was feeling his spiritual self, he came to know about a metaphysical seminar soon to be held in London. 'I should go,' he murmured with delight. But before jumping at the chance he wanted to know the thoughts of Ramesh, worldly-wise and his confidant. He rang Ramesh without losing time.

'The short answer is, "you must go",' Ramesh rang back. 'In fact, I was myself thinking to attend but unfortunately I won't be able to. And listen, you never know your luck.'

After this unequivocal endorsement Raj made up his mind to travel to London. He felt as if he was being propelled to attend the meeting.

The conference was to be held at the famous Hindu Mandir (temple) at Neasden in north-west London. Born and brought-up in a Hindu Brahman family in India, Raj's intense feeling to attend the talk was not altogether surprising. Besides, the speakers were two Indian pundits of international fame. It would also provide a little escape from the evening boredom (he lived on his own) of his Birmingham home. All he had to do was wait patiently for the opportune day: July the 2nd, 2001.

The weather forecast for the day of the meeting was a mixture of 'sunshine and showers'. After reaching London, Raj arrived at the venue from the railway station. About three quarters of an hour early. The size of the temple, visible from a distance over north-west London's sky-line, was breathtaking. There was much more to come when he entered the ornate building. The bright marble pillars (representing ancient Indian art and tradition), the chanting of mantras by priests and the fragrant smells of incense made him feel ethereal.

From a distance, Raj noticed a tall brunette in her mid-twenties standing by the side of one of the pillars. She was elegantly dressed in a cool blue summer dress. Do I know her? he wondered and gradually approached her.

'Oh, it's Amanda,' he muttered. 'What brings you here, Amanda?' Raj asked.

'I am here to attend the metaphysical conference,' she said, pointing towards the lecture hall with a beaming smile. 'I have visited this place before with my parents as they often come to this temple when stopping over in London.'

Amanda, an American, had recently completed her postgraduate course in International Relations from Birmingham University where Raj Mishra was a well-liked professor. He had perceived Amanda as amiable and candid as Americans temperamentally are.

Before the lecture began, Raj and Amanda briefly visited some sections of the temple. Amanda was especially fascinated by the prayer hall and the comings and goings of eager disciples. Then they walked together in the lecture hall. It was a stellar performance by the two speakers. Their message, clear and to the point, was enjoyed by the packed audience.

It was around 8 P.M. when they came out of the lecture hall. Just then, Amanda, looking rather apprehensive, asked: 'What are your plans for the evening Prof. Mishra?'

'Please call me Raj,' he interjected. Her line of enquiry and body language left him in no doubt that she was willing to spend more time with him that evening.

'I had thought of staying with an Indian family in Wimbledon tonight. Theirs is an open house for me. An age-old Indian way.'

'Well, if you prefer, you are welcome in my apartment in Kennsigton. It's not that far.' Amanda was looking at Raj intently. 'I am doing a little project about India and I feel you would be able to help. Do me a favour and stay, please.'

In seeking his approbation, she might have been influenced by the lively dialogue Raj had just had with the two speakers during the question and answer session of the conference. There was no disguising the fact that he was beginning to give in to her charm. In a way he was glad that he had no commitment in Birmingham the next day until later in the afternoon.

Raj nodded. 'I will be pleased to be of help and stay overnight in your apartment if that is constructive. But, I must catch the train to Birmingham tomorrow by midday at the latest,' Raj declared with a gentle tap on her shoulder.

'I am thrilled that you are going to stay. It's my responsibility to ensure that you catch your train in time.'

They settled for an Indian meal. Amanda booked a table then and there in an Indian restaurant which she said was only walking distance from her apartment.

It was a pleasant evening. Soon her white Porsche glided on rain-washed west London streets before stopping near her first-floor apartment. It was immaculate; tall trees lining both its front and back.

'My Boston-based architect father bought it for me a few years ago,' Amanda enthused. 'I like it. It is luxurious. It is also the first port of call for my parents whenever they are in London.'

A light drizzle speeded up their stroll to the restaurant. The meal was very much to their taste. Amanda also thought highly of dozens of evocative pictures hung on the restaurant's walls: Maharaja's palaces, massive temples of South India and of course, all important Agra's, The Taj Mahal.

As it was getting to midnight, Amanda and Raj, after returning to the apartment, went straight into discussion without wasting any time humming and hawing: while Raj made himself comfortable on the settee in the elegant living room, Amanda clarified the state of play relating to her project:

'I have researched a lot about India from various sources - books, internet and radio programmes,' she said with an enigmatic smile. 'I am, however, not quite clear about a few specific issues. I would like to be enlightened on those points by you - right from the horse's mouth.'

'That's fine with me,' Raj said, 'but why are you so impatient about knowing all these details about that country? Are you writing a book or something? Are you?'

'Me? Writing a book about India? Well, you never know,' she tried to explain. 'We shall have plenty of time to talk about this later, Raj.'

'I see.' Raj gave a smile of acknowledgement. He got ready to be grilled as it were: this exercise didn't worry him as he was well versed in issues dealing with India.

Their deliberation covered all manner of subjects: from India's social inequality, pollution and its caste system to the cricket-mad populace, Bollywood and the country's status as a terminus for spirituality.

Still craving to gather more facts, she enquired with the enthusiasm of a bird watcher:

'As India is fast developing, don't you think it's going to lose its old charm, customs and culture?'

'Well, this does seem to be the general anxiety and needs explaining,' Raj remarked. 'You see, India has an unrivalled knack for assimilating different cultures and the ensuing changes, and has been able to retain its past glory in spite of so many invasions and occupations. The same logic applies to the effect of its rapid growth. In any event India will continue to be a palimpsest of its bygone grandeur.'

'Finally, how would you describe India in three words?' Amanda asked.

'Diverse, mystifying, emergent,' Raj expounded with obvious relief. It didn't escape his attention that he had mesmerised Amanda by careful exposition of various points at issue.

Delighted, contented and thankful, Amanda waved her hands in the air and planted a gentle kiss on Raj's cheek.

It was dawn. Bird songs could be clearly heard signalling the climax of their exciting exchanges. Struggling to keep his eyes open and to express his thoughts properly, Raj looked at Amanda, stretched out on the long and comfortable sofa to overcome the languor, and nodded off.

It was nearly ten that mid-summer morning when Raj was woken by bright sunlight seeping through the tiny vertical slits in the curtains of the French windows. He found himself cocooned in a soft blanket. 'Oh, Amanda,' he mumbled.

During the breakfast they shared, Amanda looked thoughtful and glum. Raj wished he didn't have to leave her so soon. The taxi had arrived. After exchanging email addresses, she gave him an emotional farewell.

'I will be in touch soon,' she called as he left her apartment. Raj felt as if they had been forcefully separated.

Amanda continued to occupy Raj's mind on the train back to Birmingham. It was surprising, he reflected, that he had no prior (during Amanda's two years in Birmingham) inkling that one day he would be the focus of her attention. But then, the expression of human emotions is hardly ever straightforward: it's so variable - fleeting, meandering and unpredictable. He kept on checking her email address. He was annoyed with himself thinking their parting was one sided and casual on his part; he agonised over hardly showing any emotion. If they didn't meet again, he only had himself to blame.

That night Raj hardly slept. He kept on thinking about Amanda's thoughtful interrogations, not least her mysterious smile. Was it all pie in the sky? Would she ever contact him? And the India project? Why keep it secret? All these thoughts intrigued him.

He had interrupted sleep for several nights. He started feeling depressed. 'I am approaching forty - and Amanda? Most likely in the middle of her third decade,' he mused one morning when feeling very low.

Raj was in two minds whether to contact Amanda. He did not wish to be considered too eager or outright neglectful. He did not have to worry any longer. A week after returning from London he received this email:

Dear Raj,

I hope you reached Birmingham safely and are keeping well. I have not stopped thinking about you. I am sorry for this inordinate delay. The last few days have been very hectic. My parents have been visiting me on their way to a wider European sojourn. They are excited about the whole thing. Please let me know when we can meet. I have lots of things to tell you.

With all my love,

Amanda

Elated, Raj walked on air for the rest of the day, confident that their relationship would blossom into something wonderful.

Fast-forward to July 2003

One glorious sunny afternoon in mid-July, Raj joined the annual barbeque party at the home of Ramesh and his wife Anna. A yearly ritual and much looked forward to, the gathering was a chance to meet up with old friends and new acquaintances.

This year Raj was accompanied by Amanda and as they were warmly greeted, he introduced his new wife with much pride. After they had enjoyed the barbeque, supplemented by samosas and bhajis - with their enchanting aromas - they sat around enjoying drinks as the sun went down.

Next, Amanda slipped a book from out of her handbag like a conjurer and handed it to Raj. Its front cover featured the photograph of the Hindu temple in London.

'This is the surprise I have been working on for you. It was published only last week. I hope that it will always remind you of how we met.'

Astounded, Raj leafed through it, discovering photographs redolent of Indian life - old and new. It was a real treasure. Everyone's attention shifted from drinks to Amanda's treatise. It was admired by one and all as it was fervently passed around. It was Amanda's day - really and truly. She was enjoying everyone's attention. But, while it was a memorable event for Amanda, for Raj it was a revelation - just how had she managed to keep the whole project secret?

Back at home they were in a contemplative mood. Sitting side by side in the living room and gazing out into the starry sky, both revealed how good the last two years had been to them. Outside, their garden and the countryside beyond was bathed in glorious moonlight. The silence of the night reigned supreme. A transcendental setting. At that, the words of Ramesh were ringing in Raj's ears: you never know your luck. And, he has sensed intermittently that chime, that vibration, that period of epiphany. Ever since.

> "I do not want my house to be walled in on all sides and my windows to be stuffed. I want the cultures of all the lands to be blown about my house as freely as possible."
> *Mahatma Gandhi*

**Statue of Ganesha at Madurai Temple Complex in South India.
The illustration was drawn specially for Border Voices: Scottish Borders and
Beyond by Raghu Shukla's son, Jay Shukla.**

The Tale of a Cross Border Saint

Non fiction by *Iona Carroll*

There was once a man who became a saint. Whether or not he could have imagined that this would happen to him is a matter of conjecture and cannot be answered for the time was long ago. This man was St Cuthbert and he was born in the year 634 and died in 687 – a very long time ago indeed.

It is difficult for us in the twentieth-first century to imagine St Cuthbert's time and just as difficult to picture the man. Early biographers gave no particulars of his birth. It has been suggested that he was born in the neighbourhood of Melrose (Mailros as it was then) of lowly parentage and, as a boy he tended sheep on the hillside near the monastery. Other traditions maintain that he was the son of a well-to-do English family from North Northumberland or even that he was the son of an Irish king. Whether he was born to poor or rich parents is a matter for the scholars amongst us to puzzle over. More important, to my mind, is that this gentle man saw a vision in the sky above Melrose of heavenly angels surrounding a soul of great brightness. And this vision for Cuthbert was the body of his mentor, St Aidan, the Bishop of Lindisfarne - who had died that very night. Cuthbert believed that this was so and it was this belief that changed his life.

Here was a young man looking after some sheep and I doubt that he would have been expecting to see a vision in the sky. He was brought up a Christian and it had been recorded earlier that his prayers saved some monks from being swept out to sea on a raft. So the seeds of a devout life might already have been sown in him before his life-changing experience on the hillside above Melrose. While still a child and living with his foster mother, Kenswith, his future as a Bishop was foretold to him. This prediction appears to have had a lasting effect on his character and, perhaps influenced by the holiness of the monastic community at Melrose as well, his vision on the hillside was not totally unexpected.

Again, whether he rushed off immediately to the nearby monks to announce his vocation to the religious life or whether, as some scholars suggest, he spent time as a soldier in the service of the King of Northumberland cannot be verified. All we know is that this young man was so convinced after his vision that the monastic life was to be his destiny. This was a time of great religious controversy between the Celtic and the Roman influences of the early Christian church in Britain. The Melrose monks adhered to the Celtic tradition and it is here that Cuthbert become known for his piety and devotion. We know that he spent the next thirteen years or so with the Melrose monks. He was greatly influenced by Boisil, the prior at Melrose who became his teacher and friend. Cuthbert's reputation for holiness and learning was evident and it is possible that he went with the founding party of monks to a new monastery at Ripon and was made guest master. there. Expelled from Ripon when he refused to accept the Roman monastic tradition, he returned to Melrose and was appointed the Prior in 661 after the death of Boisil.

However, in 664 the Synod of Whitby decided to approve the Roman method and it appears that Cuthbert went along with that decision. At about thirty years of age he moved to Lindisfarne – the Holy Island – and lived there for ten years. At Lindisfarne he was a very active missionary, renowned for his spiritual healing, compassion and cheerful disposition. In those transforming years of establishing Christianity in the British Isles, Cuthbert would have been a highly regarded exponent of the new faith. However, he desired to live a life of contemplation and, in 676 he was granted his wish. As a contemplative, he became known for his great austerity and it appears that it was with much reluctance on his part, and after constant persuasion from both Church and King that he finally agreed to leave his hermitage to become Bishop of Lindisfarne. He was consecrated at York in 685. His remaining years were spent tirelessly preaching, evangelizing and travelling extensively. Feeling the approach of death he retired to his hermitage on the Inner Farne where he died on March 20th 687. But Cuthbert's story did not end there and it is possibly what happened after his death that is as intriguing as was his life!

He was buried on Lindisfarne and it was here that people came to pray at his grave. Many miracles of healing were claimed and, according to the monks of Lindisfarne, Cuthbert was now a saint as the miracles were so numerous. He was called 'The Wonder-worker of England'. At the eleventh anniversary of his death the monks of Lindisfarne re-opened his coffin to discover not a skeleton but a perfectly preserved body. Almost immediately, his tomb was associated with even more miraculous events. This gentle man, who as a boy had once cared for sheep on a hillside, was now the object of veneration and pilgrimage.

During the Viking raids of 875 the monks took Cuthbert's remains with them. This had been the saint's instruction if the monks ever had cause to leave Lindisfarne. For seven years the monks wandered around the North of England carrying Cuthbert with them. Incredibly, for over a hundred years Cuthbert's body rested at various locations including Chester-le Street and Ripon. After the Norman Conquest in 1066, Cuthbert's remains, together with the head of the warrior King, St Oswald, were placed in a specially built shrine at the newly built Durham Cathedral. According to legend, the body of St Cuthbert and the head of St Oswald were still perfectly preserved when the coffin was opened yet again.

With the Dissolution of the Monasteries in 1534, Cuthbert's tomb was plundered. It was reported that his body had still not decayed. In 1827 the saint was disturbed once more. A coffin was opened which appeared to be

the same one that the monks had carried with them almost a thousand years before. Within lay a skeleton holding a St Cuthbert's cross. Finally, the grave was opened again in 1899 and expert examination proved that the body of St Cuthbert had been mummified and it was most probably that of the saint. The remains were eventually re-interred and marked by a plain gravestone with the name Cuthbertus. It had been Cuthbert's wish that he be buried at Durham.

It is perhaps appropriate to end this short narrative about St Cuthbert – 'the wonder-worker saint' – with a very twenty-first century tribute to the man. In 2012 the Gospel of St Cuthbert was purchased by the British Library for £9m and will remain in Britain for the nation. The library acquired the Gospel in partnership with Durham University and Durham Cathedral and it is to be displayed equally at the library and in the North East. This greatly treasured book, buried with St Cuthbert in the twelfth century, will hold a place of great honour in Durham Cathedral Priory in the twentieth-first. The Gospel has survived as much as St Cuthbert himself and is the stuff of legend as well. It will rest with him in Durham.

St Cuthbert's influence has spread around the world to Australia, New Zealand, North America and Europe. In 1987 widespread celebrations marked the 1300th anniversary of his death and his reputation as one of Britain's most charismatic of saints is assured.

In 2011, a solid oak Celtic cross was erected in front of the St Cuthbert's Church at Melrose. It was sculpted by Ember Hall.

Front face - The St Cuthbert's cross is featured in the middle, with Melrose Abbey to the right and the Eildons & Tweed on the left. The view of the Eildons & Tweed is that from Scott's view, part of St Cuthbert's way. The Celtic pattern is from the priest's robe, on the top vertical, with a mimicked extended version upside down on the bottom vertical. Then spaced round the ringed section are Celtic ovals featured on both sides of the cross.

Back face - Again St Cuthbert's cross in the centre, moving out to the Celtic squares then images of the Melrose Abbey Pilgrims badge on either side, the Christian symbol of the Fish and below the X P is another symbol used for "Christ" featured on the top vertical, and a Celtic symbol on the long vertical.

Photographs © Copyright Ember Hall

A Man an Hiz Dug: a wee Embra tale

Fiction by *Tom Bryan*

Shuggie wiz awfy fond o hiz dug Jenni, ken. Fed hur better scran than he fed tae himsel. Nae lang since Ah last seen Shug. He wiz worriet seek aboot hiz dug, aboot no bein able tae feed hur an aa. Mind, Shug didnae fancy girls, jist Jenni, ken.

Seen Shuggie sittin oan thi rail o North Bridge, like oan a cuddy, ken, facin the gowpin crood. Ah seen fur thi furst time thit Shug's een were thi same cauld grey as thi paint oan thi Bridge. Grey Castle, Grey Scott Monument an Shug's grey een keekin oot tae Portobelly Pooer Station. Jenni wiz lickin Shug's heid. Aye, Shuggie nivver shavit, mindit ye o yon cairtoon Scooby Doo, thit glaikit yin, ken, wi they lang chin hairs hingin doon? Shuggie lookit at me wi een like frozen slavers. Thi licht had gaan oot---like naebiddy hame, ken? Then he jist liftit hiz left leg, like a cowboy an Ah moved tae grab Shuggie, but he jist slid ower thi edge, slow-motion like. Ah haird Jenni barkin aa thi way doon. Polis sez she landit oan Shug, brakin hur ain faa. Dug wiz fine, ken. She's mine thi noo. But she wullnae gang onywhaur near North Bridge. Mind, Ah cannae gang thit wey mysel, thit grey Bridge thi colour o Shug's deid een peerin oot tae Portobelly - whaur thi Pooer Station used tae be.

Poem by *Tom Murray*

New York New York

Hotel doormen speaking out of the corner of their mouths
Like every New York film you ever saw.

Central Park, joggers jogging,
Talkers talking politics.
Vendors making a buck.
Packs of pampered pets
Walking their walkers.

Lincoln Centre, an orchestra morphing
Into Glenn Millar style
While students pretend to study in the midday sun.

Me spilling my coffee
Clicking the digital camera
Of my mind
Telling tales
Of a less hurried landscape.

Thinking.
This is the life.
It's good to be a writer.

Polarity

A Sonnet by *Vee Freir*

A slab of cloud strands the Scottish Borders,
sleeting on the green-and-brown tartan fields,
mud-filled and water-logged. Sheep find shelter
by rain-soaked hedgerows, a skeleton shield
against the storm. While crows, their wings outspread,
wheel on the edge of the wind and delight
in this violent weather; black warheads.
I stay safe surrounded by Border granite
and reminisce of sunny southern climes,
of the Eastern Cape; sat on the seafront
under the blue, blue sky of summertime
and sun-edged cumulus high and distant.
Those swallows sweeping along your skyline,
the same that cross the sea and visit mine.

Non Fiction by *Gunther Alexander*

A Traveller's return from a Trip to Tibet

Diary extract of a journey the author made from a Tibetan Town called Dengke to the regional 'city' Yushu earlier this year.

We've left Dengke and climbed up the beautiful valley, past the picnic spot where we talked on Skype that time. The mountains covered in snow at the valley's head makes the day seem serene. We climb higher and higher, more beautiful scenery, past yaks and camps as we head for the snow line.

The snow edges downward, or we upward, and the 4x4 labours and we begin to slither on the corners. The reality begins to enter the car, we are alone save for one set of tyre marks in the ice covered snow, several thousand meters up on a pass that no one uses. The girls' jabbering in the back begins to take on a different tone and then silence gradually falls as we all concentrate on the road.

The road levels and the scenery is beautiful. We are passengers, its delightful. We've found voices again and live in a false universe. I ask the driver to stop so we can take photos. He rebukes, sharply. He's still in the land of reality, of the remaining five hour drive across this landscape.

We climb again, thankful for the rocky protuberances on the road which seem to give us some grip. We are looking at rocks the size of dogs which the ice and sun have slipped from their sleepy leashes high up on the mountainside.

We reach another crest, finding a snow covered tent, surrounded by smoke breathing yaks. Scenery like Rannoch Moor yet vast enough to fill the sky. A calf, unduly impatient to be born, snuggles up to Mum wishing it were back inside. It's too cold to be born into this life. A scarecrow, face covered with cloth, overcoat upon overcoat, moves as swiftly as the stiff clothes allow, and then I recognise a human, incongruous in this environment, even more so than a scarecrow.

We're onto the brown stuff, safe at last. Yet mud is just as bad as ice! We slither occasionally, the driver sharp and tense but the road is level, nothing can happen now. We hope. We seem to fly, the speedo reaching 10 mph, the road reminding me of the top of Glencoe with Aonach Eagach on the left and Bidean nam Bian on the right. A bridge across a wide burn shouts out a 5t limit, yet we all know the road was built for tanks. Above, the lammergeier circle lazily and I wonder about the car in front.

We're dropping again, the yak herds grow, no longer guarded by scarecrows. Human figures with baskets on their backs collect yak dung like pony-besotted teenagers keeping their paddocks clean and worm free. Here of course dung is fuel and fuel gives life.

Pony saddled herdsmen intrude, riding around the side of the herd, husbanding or worm grass collecting? It's impossible to say.

Faster now, we reach 30mph, the jabbering rising with the speed. Mud intrudes and brings the speed back down again. Still we've made progress, a little.

The road, fickle as always, improves, hard core straining the tyres. The grass greener now, sprouts sheep and with it tents like patches of snow along the sunny side of the hill, the shadow side still gripped in tundra and grey.

The road crawls by; milepost 57 gives way to 56. From where, to where? I peer at the map and remain ignorant, there's nothing marked for hundreds of miles.

We pass camps, washing hanging in the sun, bright and cheerful, changes our mood. We laugh, we're making progress, the ice and mud behind us, for now.

Bandits, with facemasks, on blanket-covered motorbikes appear in front. Waving cheerfully, faces unseen, off to join the scarecrows perhaps.

More and more, families on bikes out along the road to find luxury by digging for worm grass, that elixir of life for HIV sufferers.

Wire from fences is strewn along the edge; yaks obviously impervious to its warning have dragged and mangled it. Such futility in this barren landscape.

A ruined mill on the far side of the river, that powered some long lost crushing device, brought riches for a while before dying with the market. Or spent, perhaps, having spewed its riches out.

The ground is so hard that ubiquitous telegraph poles are built on islands of rock not sunk into the earth. Civilisation begins to intrude. Poles, serving no obvious purpose save standing to attention for the weary traveller, sprout buzzard nests, giant birds sitting on eggs glowering as we pass, hoping to hatch just as the temperature rises, praying not to miscalculate.

Fences now standing hopeful of a better life than earlier wire, stand in military fashion yet at ease. Even here, attention is too rigid in this landscape.

A township on the horizon? The valley broadening into a plateau, puddles no longer coated with ice, tyres no longer crunching through. Poles, now safely buried, hint at a softer life around.

The township, a 'nomad' township, block houses, arranged in lines. Industrial units without eyes or features appear as we approach from the sunless side, utilitarian, no luxury to waste on windows and doors in this environment.

Mud intrudes again, we slow down.

Suddenly, by surprise, a checkpoint. All are shocked, us and even the police youths themselves. No one knows what to do. We shouldn't be here, they shouldn't be here, no one said there would be a checkpoint here at all. We all mumble, apologetically, confusion reigns. We drive on.

We round a corner, happy, happy that we've got through, happy seeing that they were guarding the beginnings of tarmac. Black stuff so delightful, beautiful, smooth. For a while.

We doze, the landscape unbecoming until at last we reach Soushou, county town and local king. It was to this court that Dengke's mayor was summoned to answer for the impetuosity of our arrival without papers or permission. Four hours drive for a bollocking! Get a life.

Wire posts are standing to attention, a courtesy to the District Governor perhaps?

We climb again, towards Amballa, asphalt dying under the ice and snow, leaving gaping holes which rip the tyres.

We pass a foal, scarce days old, back covered with lambskin, one dying so that one can live.

The road flattening, mind drifts away, sleep.

A police patrol brings gasps, silence then relief. They drive past, we drive past.

Smiles from nomad villages greet us. The road has twisted and we see the sunny side. Same buildings, what a difference a smile makes.

The bridge, so strong, complete with 5t sign, swept away by tidal forces as river lurched to the sea. The road diverts, wider and wider as successive lorries seek to gain a foothold on the tundra. We bump and tense, as wheels bite, grip and move forward. We move again.

Another 'town' appears, built against the hillside monastery. The monastery large and growing, sponsored by foreigners, for a Lama far away, with cult like following. Pilgrims circle the monastery below seeking blessing, lammergeiers above seeking food. Sky burials most mornings, death bringing life.

Good tar lifts our spirits again. Along the roadside long pits, where vehicles now excavate the soil, feeding buildings and walls, industrial in its scale, well almost.

Another checkpoint springs up. We know about this one. Smoke rising from the stack, we sneak up, its still early and, like the thieves we are, steal by, permits to be here stolen by our presence.

A buzzard, or even eagle on a pole. Photos please? But driver, knowing he has to come back, is impatient and I don't press.

The tundra, no longer brown. Green shimmering through with sparkles of white and yellow flowers. We too are impatient with far to go.

Pica sitting on the road, bemused by our presence, scuttles away at the last minute. An oncoming car, looking like Cooper after Ali, waves a cheery grin at us. It's been in a landslide, screen white, doors dented, wheel hubs pressed into the wheels. A sobering thought, we're quiet again, for a while.

We catch up with an army lorry, happy to have company, yet realising what company, awaiting a permit inspection. Its arrogance makes overtaking difficult, but we manage and move away. See a 5t bridge and wonder what the extra fifteen ton will do. Perhaps it only applies to civilian lorries.

We're on a plateau again, the same, different, how many levels are there before heaven? Eyes are weary, drop off, driver awake, I hope.

Mountains in a snow-covered ring all around us, beautiful as we travel towards them.

As we get to the next bridge we wonder how we will get through the next checkpoint, reputed to be bad. Stillness reigns as we drive. We see smoke, lots of it and smile. The asphalteers are repairing the road and have their wok of tar on a makeshift fire near the hut. The fumes have obviously won. No one to stop us. Someone smiles, we all smile, asphalteers and travellers, perhaps they know what they have done, probably not. We sneak under the unmanned beam, just clearance enough for the 4x4. I wonder what the army lorry will do.

We're making good progress again but the road is winding. Wendy in the back complains and we stop as a red and white duck flies by.

Suddenly it dawns on us that the mountains are where we are going. We're climbing once more. Rivers garner ice again and roadside puddles look bejewelled.

Nomads assembling tents, women hammering tent pegs home with rocks. Why carry a hammer! Hasty repairs with red, blue and white plastic sheeting. Ground churned up by yaks and tyres.

Snow partly, freshly fallen, freshly melted. The snow that delayed Dr Ray last week? Probably. The pass 4,700m clear. Far on the hillside above ant-like figures are quick to exploit the uncovered ground and pick away to find the worm grass. Years of salaries depend on success.

Page 58

The road drops down, the girls squeal with delight. I look at the drop and pray, then redouble my efforts as we overtake blindly.

Squealing changes tone. Wendy car sick again, just makes it. We scramble out taking pictures. A red-breasted bird poses for photos, or perhaps pickings from Wendy's breakfast.

Off again, we drive, level with a lark hovering there, from his perspective hundreds of feet up, Wendy wishes I could have photographed it.

We drop quickly, 30km signs ignored. I wish, try praying again. It worked, we approach a bottom. Wendy sprawled in the back almost comatose, pale and ill.

A nomad camp with prayer pole and flags streaming in all directions, colourful, like a giant helicopter ready for take off.

Many more calves now, now that its greener, warmer, perhaps better sheltered.

A red lorry, shiny, new, comes towards us breaking the monotony. We all wave, happy not to be alone.

We pass a camp by a stream. A lonely old crone standing in the river, bent double, barefoot, looking for stones. Can't she feel anything? Did your necklace come from here? Am I proud to have helped or have I exploited her? I don't know. but feel better for not having haggled.

We're dropping quite quickly again, ears popping like firecrackers down towards Yushu. Earthquake town.

The trees here sprout leaves, its as though the mountains are squeezing them out!

Yushu. How do I begin to describe it? The town doesn't exist any more save a statue in the middle. Its a giant dust-covered building site. The entire population living in blue tent communities relocated away from the centre. Its a tragedy, its amazing.

I'm back in the Borders now and drink the green landscape. Each turn on the roads yielding more and more green. Like an addict I just can't drink enough.

Uncle Billy – The First Eco-Warrior

Non Fiction by *Carol Norris*

I was brought up living with Uncle Billy who was born in 1912. All his life he had lived and worked in an industrial area midway between Nottingham and Derby by the valley of the River Erewash, which once had the distinction of being the most polluted river in Europe, but he longed for the golden age of rurality, the old days. 'In them days', things were different. In compensation for a lost paradise, he husbanded with loving care a small suburban plot called 186 Brookhill Street.

In late May, when it was 'warm' probably ' 'ot' and therefore 'muggy', forget-me-nots would be out in blue profusion with the delphiniums, the fuchsias, the apple blossom, the flags and irises, the flocks, the lavender, the old English rambling roses, the curiously clipped yews, the peonies, the scabius, the honeysuckle, and the lilac and lilies.

'If yu want any flags, yu can 'ave some of 'em if you want'. He grew clumps of Erigeron from a seed dropped by a bird, apple trees from apple cores, peach trees from peach stones. He saved the seeds from all the delphiniums and cowslips. He grafted old roses, and grew Guelder roses from the seeds.

There was never a weed in the garden, or rather; there was one, left to flourish in splendid isolation – either as an idiosyncratic tribute to the weeds, or as an ironic gesture of eccentricity. I never knew which, as all Billy would say was 'Aye, well, there is one ovva there - I'll 'ave t' gerrit awt'.

A rusted, completely holed, and functionally useless wheelbarrow stood at the end of the garden, not to be filled with trailing decorative plants as a garden feature - but simply preserved as a monument to the Iron Foundry (lately demised) of Stanton Ironworks and a tribute simply to being old and worn with careful use. Thus, every screw, every part used piece of timber, every nut and bolt, every lock, every old gas fire, oil lamp, oilcloth, curtains, a seventy year old rag carpet made by Grandma; all brown paper, used envelopes, every used matchstick, the completely organic gas stove in the kitchen, as old as time, every gas vent and orifice of which, congealed and mostly concealed in fossilised black gunge, and working with twenty percent or less efficiency, - all saved, not simply to hoard, but as a monument to principle, frugality, the veneration of craftsmanship and the daily toil, the abhorrence of waste, of squander and consumerism.

Billy loved things that were good, solid and well made. He paid for a tractor to be bought for his three year old great-nephew three weeks before he died, and not liking the cheap nastiness of the plastic, walked ten miles there and back to save the bus fare, to buy a much more solid, heavy and expensive one. At the time of carrying it back, he must have been very ill but thought it worth the great effort it must have cost him.

In the past he had slowly carved solid brass aeroplanes and made silver plated wire and steel jewellery with long labour. He was a fitter by trade and could work with metal and solder but he favoured wood and was always comforted and reassured when something was made of solid wood.

'Wood, Aye'.

Above all, he loved the great ocean liners of the past, the "Doric" and "Georgic", indeed all of them, their steam engines and teak decks. He made a working model of the White Star twin screw liner "Doric", incorporating a steam engine within, which went on display for a while in a local shop window.

As the years passed, Uncle Billy began to look himself like something wooden, a very old, warped, twisted vine trellis, sinewy, coiled in on itself and slowly shrinking.

In the last months with increasing illness, he no longer could maintain his garden and would point through the living room window with spindle fingers, his grey face gaping at the void of the abandoned garden, a blackened relic staring at extinction.

'Can yo smell gas?' suddenly, twisting round and down to the gas fire with a familiar movement.

We bent down, first one and then the other.

'No, Billy'.

Later, he bent over the dresser.

'Can yo smell gas?'

'No, Billy'.

He was, in his own all-encompassing word, 'Bad'.

That meant a generality of illnesses which tended to be fatal but in general, with him, implied one definitely specific illness for which he could use no word other than 'Bad', especially when used in the double repetition, 'Bad. Bad' to mean only one thing, the completely unspeakable word, cancer. And cancer was the cause of the canker's well which he was now carrying within him as a result of obstruction of the large bowel.

The next day he gained enough strength to put his hat and coat on, blackened world-weary objects that they were, and walked with us down the next side street to the Sub Post Office. On the way, he leant over a low garden wall and peered into the little garden abloom with roses.

'Can yo smell gas?' 'Sweetish smell.' 'Gas!'

'No we can't.'

But a canary would have fallen dead at his feet. That gas was methane, and it did not come from the gas main or any leaking gas appliance.

It came from him - a blockage deep in the fundament with gases streaming ever upwards from the black seams of the deep, reminiscent of the gases and steam erupting from the bowels of the sinking Titanic with great explosions.

The morning of his death the undertaker came down to us from the bedroom where Billy lay, holding up a greeting card I had sent to Billy, a painting of the "Olympic", sister ship of the "Titanic", steaming out of Liverpool.

'I am the Secretary of the Nottingham Branch of The Titanic Preservation Society.'

How we laughed and laughed, the peels of laughter rising up to Billy where he lay.

I sensed at that moment a rare broad smile passing over Billy's face at such perfect timing.

The Model of SS Doric made by Uncle Billy

The field of Waterloo

Poem by *Bridget Khursheed*

Inspecting Vandeleur's brigade
the 11th Light Dragoons:
local men found there include
a Corporal Ralph Darling
a dark-haired Northumbrian
attentive to his camp follower
their bairn being in illness
until called over to describe
the ride forward to stuff the hole
as he put it on the left flank.
Blucher found the gate barred.
A shepherd's son from Ancroft
Moor he had roamed
the Peninsular and met his lady
there. We discussed
the size of Cheviot ravens
in comparison to these
that cleaned the battlefield.
He would not mind sheep again
he said. And I envied him
his new path.
A shepherd soldier
and myself in the uniform
of Edinburgh and lame.
We smoked a little
and toasted our Borderlands.
Parting, he offered me two cuirasses
one with the shell hole
still unfiled. And I took them
from him for a good price
I thought until rumbling on to Paris
I found them piled for sous
the length of the road.

First published in the Irish magazine *The Shop*

Fiction by *Marie-Claire Dibbern*

Leaving Traquair

Leaving Traquair is inspired by the real life story of the remarkable Father William Wallace chaplain to the Stuarts of Traquair from 1821 - 1846.

'You must prepare to meet your maker, Father Wallace.'

The old priest stirred beneath the counterpane and whispered, his voice emerging in rasping breaths.

'Who bids you bring these tidings, Andrew?'

'Your physicians Father – they can do no more.'

The young priest leaned closer to hear the old man's instructions. He felt the patient's hot breath on his cheek and grimaced at the fetid smell.

'You will hear my confession Father Andrew?' His voice was barely audible.

The old priest wheezed and shifted under the covers in a fruitless bid to relieve the pain which racked his bones and reduced his once mighty frame to little more than a cadaver.

Somewhere a door creaked as Lady Stuart entered carrying the lighted candles for the sacred rites. Dimly William Wallace perceived his hostess whose family he had ministered to these last twenty five years. Whether a trick of the light, his failing eyesight or the sedative, he fancied he was regarded not by the solemn countenance of her ladyship but another lady, not seen in fifty years or more.

'Mither, is that you?' whispered the old man.

'Aye, Wullie whae else wid it be laddie?' her cold slim hands brushed his head and brow.

Anxiously he levered himself up

'Mither, what news of Robert?'

The lady's face clouded over

'Son, why dae ye grieve ma heirt more than it already is? Ye ken yer brither died fighting thon American rebels. It was aye the same with the Wallaces o' Huntly. Aye seeking excitement, aye travelling....so far from hame.'

She turned away sadly and before he could ask her more she swept out the door, leaving nothing but a glimpse over her red skirts.

'Hush now, rest,' a voice soothed.

Colours and memories flooded in. Now it was the purple robes of the Bishop of Douay mingling with the candles and incense. In the distance the sound of Gregorian chants filled the cathedral as the bishop pronounced the final blessing on the newly ordained priests.

'God be with you. God speed William.' The abbe gripped the horse's bridle while the mare snorted and pawed the ground as if anxious to be gone.

'I hate to leave... I feel... a coward...'

'Napoleon's army is but an hour's ride from here. They will slaughter any priest they find. You must hurry! When God wills it, you will return.'

'And you?'

'I am an old man now, but you are young and still have the Lord's work to do. Be gone!' he slapped the mare's rump.

'What happened to you abbé?" the old man stirred, feverishly plucking at the bed clothes,

'Hush now, you must rest, you are very weak. Shall I hear your confession now?'

'Dom Francisco, is that you?' He tightened his grip on the young man's arm.

'No, Father Wallace, it's Father Andrew here. You are safe in Traquair. It's 1844. The tyrant Bonaparte is long dead. France is safe. Spain is safe.'

This seemed to settle him and he sank back onto his pillows. Not France. Not Spain. Scotland. Safe in the Borderlands.

It hadn't always been so. The Stuarts of Traquair kept the Faith and paid dearly for it. They will gain their reward in heaven.

And the poor, what of the poor?

'The poor are always with us,' says the Lord. 'All we can do is love them.'

Father Wallace tried to love them. To be sure sometimes it was a rough kind of wooing but the flock must be protected from the wickedness that stalks them, as the wolf stalks the new born lambs.

The poor! So many wretches, nowhere to worship, no one to hear their confessions, so far from family and home.

The Lady Stuart entreated him to rest but he couldn't rest while the Abbe and Dom Francisco were dead. So out he rode out from Traquair to Peebles, to Hawick and to Galashiels. He never relented until he raised the money to build the church in Hawick although seven years it took him.

'Father Wallace, you are seventy now, you have done enough. I fear you will become ill,' chided the Lady Stuart.

Of course he couldn't stop, after Hawick there was Kelso, so pathetic these famine refugees. Disdained and despised these Irish, mistrusted and shunned. Who would care for them, protect them, baptise them and bury them?

To Abbotsford and Springwood from the Stuarts of Traquair to the Kerrs of Huntlyburn. Old families keeping the Faith. Few could resist his charm. He would get his church.

'Father Wallace. The good Lord himself could not have done more. Any man of seventy seven is permitted to retire. I implore you for the sake of your health stop now!'

She should have known better – hadn't her beloved mother also tried to slow him down?

'Father Wallace will die in harness,' he once overheard the groom say, but what use was it sitting in a castle waiting to die?

It wasn't Napoleon's army or a Presbyterian riot which did for him but a late November Borders downpour. Brought him to this familiar bed chamber, this final journey.

'Father, let me hear your confession and give you absolution.'

Too late. He had gone to his Maker by way of Huntly, Douay, Valladolid and Traquair.

'Te absolvo. In Nomine Patris et Filii et Spiritus Sancti. Amen.'

Historical Note
Father William Wallace was born in 1768 in Huntly Aberdeenshire. After an eventful life serving as a Catholic priest and distinguished teacher first in Douay, Nothern France and then Valladollid, Spain whence he had to flee for his life, he arrived aged fifty -three at Traquair. Appointed chaplain he spent the next twenty-five years ministering not only to the Stuarts of Traquair but also to the scattered Catholic population who at that period comprised both greatest and most wretched in society.

After his dangerous sojourn in Europe he couldn't have been blamed if he had settled for the more tranquil existence of 'a country house priest'. However seeking a quiet life was not it seemed in his nature.

In his seventies he was riding out all over the Borders ministering to his scattered flock. After seven long years of fundraising he built the first RC church in the Borders since the Reformation. It's successor still stands in Buccleuch St Hawick and is dedicated to St Mary and St David.

Aged seventy-eight he did the same again in Kelso. It fell to his successor Fr Patrick Taggart to complete the project which he did with the help of the Hope-Scotts of Abbotsford and the Scott-Douglas family of Springwood Kelso among others.The original wooden structure was burnt down in an anti-Irish riot in 1856. It's successor the Immaculate Conception (St Mary's) was consecrated in 1858 and is located opposite the modern day Kelso High School.

For more details on this extraordinary man please refer to " A Furnished Room", The History of a Parish by Joe McMenemy. Copies can be obtained from St Mary's RC Church, Bowmont Street, Kelso.

Berwick-upon-Tweed

Non Fiction by *Eileen Thornton*

A few miles south of Kelso lies the bustling market town of Berwick-upon-Tweed. Looking across the Tweed from the south bank, the town takes on an almost fairytale appearance as it rises steeply up the narrow cobbled streets. At the top, the spire of the Guild Hall can be seen towering grandly over the picturesque red tiled roofs. All seeming to reflect an air of tranquility. Yet because of its strategic position on the north side of the River Tweed, this town has been fought over by Scotland and England for centuries. It has actually changed hands between these two great nations no less than thirteen times.

After a Scottish victory at Carham-upon-Tweed in 1018, the River Tweed was declared the boundary, putting Berwick firmly on Scottish soil. During the following years, the town prospered and was made a Scottish Royal Burgh by King David I in 1120 along with Roxburgh, Edinburgh and Selkirk. These good times might have continued if it had not been for the untimely invasion from England in 1296.

King Edward I plundered the town and, deciding it would make an ideal military base, he built walls to protect it from further Scottish attacks. Nevertheless, Berwick was retaken the following year, after William Wallace's victory at Stirling Bridge, only to be lost again in 1298. And so it went on until in 1482 when the Duke of Gloucester, who later became the infamous Richard III, finally regained Berwick for England.

A further interesting point in the town's history is that after 1482, Berwick was given the special status of being a 'Free Burgh' and was mentioned separately in any important documents. For instance, when the Crimean War began, all official documents stated, Victoria, Queen of Great Britain, Ireland, Berwick-upon-Tweed and all the British Dominions. However when the war ended, due to an oversight, the Paris Peace Treaty failed to mention Berwick-upon-Tweed. Therefore technically the town remained at war with Russia until 1966, when a Soviet official made a special visit to the town thus proving that peace prevailed.

Today the walls of the town, rebuilt during the reign of Elizabeth I, stand as a monument to Berwick's turbulent past. Topped with a grassy mound and footpath, people may take a pleasant stroll and enjoy a whole new perspective of the town.

The one and a half mile walk passes the various strongholds and also crosses Scotsgate, the old, narrow gateway to the town from the north. At one time the Great North Road (A1) ran through the town and under this gateway causing congestion at times. Now a bypass takes the A1 traffic away from the town centre.

Just outside the gateway once stood the medieval church of St. Mary, from which Marygate, the main street of the town, takes its name. Marygate is filled with bright modern shops, which work hand in hand with the twice-weekly Charter Market dating back to 1302.

Near the bottom of Marygate is Eastern Lane. Here, the old meets the new in the form of The Maltings Theatre and Arts Centre. The building also has a café, which looks down onto the older part of Berwick. From the panoramic windows, there are bird's eye views of the river and its bridges, as well as the rooftops of the buildings below. Their tall chimneys are reminiscent of Mary Poppins' London.

There are many fine buildings in the town, but the Guild Hall, more commonly known as the Town Hall that stands at the bottom of Marygate, is the most notable. Built in the middle of the 18th century by the Berwick Guild, the Hall has presided over the town for over two hundred years.

In the past, the building was not only used for important functions, but was also the town gaol. Some of the cells still survive today, as have the irons used to restrain prisoners. Because of its central point, the Hall is now used for charity coffee mornings as well as for business functions.

A stone's throw from the Town Hall is Wallace Green, which is said to take its name from William Wallace, as one of his dismembered limbs was displayed here after his execution in 1305. Furthermore, tucked quietly away in one corner of the green, is The Holy Trinity Parish Church.

The church, built during the times of Cromwell, is unusual in that it has neither a steeple nor a bell. It is for this reason that the Town Hall bell is rung each Sunday to summon the congregation to the services. This some-times causes confusion to the town's visitors, as they believe the Town Hall to be the church.

Another notable feature of the town is its three bridges. The oldest dates back to the early 17th century and replaced a series of wooden bridges crossing the Tweed at the same spot. While making his way to London in

1604 to accept the throne of England after the death of Elizabeth I, it is said that King James VI, fearing for his safety, declared that a new stronger bridge should be built before he returned to Edinburgh.

This bridge, now known as 'The Old Bridge', took the A1 traffic until The Royal Tweed Bridge was opened in1928 by the Prince of Wales, later to become Edward VIII. In recent years the bridge has been reinforced to take today's modern traffic.

However the largest of the three bridges was built to carry the railway from London to Edinburgh. On completion, it was Queen Victoria, who declared the bridge open. Robert Stephenson, who built the Royal Border Bridge, demolished most of Berwick Castle to make way for the station. The station platform now occupies the spot where the Great Hall of the castle once stood. Reputedly, it was in the Great Hall in 1292 that Edward I favoured John Balliol over Robert Bruce to take the throne of Scotland. Four years later he was to regret his decision, as Balliol decided to take Berwick for himself. It was this act that began the long series of wars.

Just to the north of Berwick is the magnificent viewpoint of Halidon Hill. It was here that, after a long battle in 1333, Edward III of England regained Scotland. The viewpoint looks down to the River Tweed and the town beyond. On a clear day the Cheviots can be seen in the distance, as can the castles of Lindisfarne and Bamburgh.

Finally Berwick is not only famous for its salmon, but also for the herd of swans that gather under the bridges searching for food thrown to them by tourists. A few years ago the Swan and Wildlife Trust was set up to help care for them, should they run into difficulties. Since then a local vet received an OBE from the Queen for his dedication to the swans and other wildlife in the area.

Quilts in the Drakkensberg mountains

"high in the Drakkensberg mountains
is a viewpoint called God's Window"

God's Window

Poem by *Pim Claridge*

high in the Drakkensberg mountains
is a viewpoint called God's Window

in the wind the quilts had flapped upon the loop of line
and colours glowed as if songs were stitched in every flower, bird
or tree as they waited to be sold...
the mountains faded blue on blue into the
shining distance and the wind blew warm with summer..
the rocky path was steep and along the edge the stag's moss grew
as it does at home in scottish hills, and higher still the flowers
grew brighter and a scent of herbs prevailed...
then a gap between the rocks and a rail on which to lean
and catch your breath, and then you see it, stretched
beyond the cliffs, forests and more forests..the wonder
of the space, the hugeness and the silence
hit every sense and nerve I had....
I looked down to the distant valley floor,
then up to the haze of the blue edged hills,
and heard the waterfall drop
psalms to the churning pool below..
and knew that this was indeed
God's Window
and his Kingdom,
had come....

Published in *Shadow on the Sand*,
see www.pimclaridge.com for further information.

Non Fiction by *Rosalie Saunders*

Ramunia

'This other Eden, Ramunia!', was the entry in our family's Visitors book written by Zoe Benn, headmistress of the Westernhay school, Malacca, where my brother boarded. Our bungalow on stilts stood on a jewel of a tropical beach in what in the fifties was Johore State, Malaya. It faced a short stretch of water over to Changi in Singapore. We were the only Scots in Ramunia. However there were often visits from fellow Borderers serving with the KOSB or Special Branch, or Scots from Princess Mary's Own Gurkha Regiment. It was the time of the troubles, so we also had visits from the Royal Malayan Navy, New Zealand Air Force, the Police, Customs, Japanese Businessmen, people with strange titles like 'Chief Food Denial Inspector' and as my father was Mining Superintendant of the Bauxite mine in Ramunia, the Inspector of Mines .

When we lived in Bukit Besi in Trengganu State, my mother was a soft touch for taking on people's pets when they went back home on furlough or didn't return. We had had dogs, monkeys, slow loris, mouse deer, a foul mouthed mynah bird, some stray cats, as well as parakeets rescued from the bazaar. Ramunia was no different! However this was the largest addition to the Brydon menagerie so far! Josephine, known as 'Joey' was a four foot Himalayan bear, sometimes called a 'Sun bear'. Unfortunately her mother had been shot before it was discovered that she had a cub. Joey had dark brown fur with a splash of orange under her chin, and had very long claws. She was mainly good natured although one day she sat on my nine year old brother. He had to be rescued before he could get up from floundering under her weight.

Friday was the Muslim Holy Day and Joey's favourite day as my father would bring her a weekly treat. A huge enclosure had been built for Joey with her own house on stilts within it for sleeping quarters. Pop would approach her with hands behind his back. Joey would see him through the fencing, and rise up, drooling at the mouth, as he produced a Mars Bar, one for each paw. How she loved them! She also loved a gunny sack, which she rubbed rather like a child does with a 'sookie blanket'. At that time we had an Indian cook who didn't like the bear and would sometimes tease her by pulling away her comforter. One day he did this not realising that the gate to her abode was not secured properly. With a growl Joey pushed it open. In two ticks she was free and chased her tormentor round the house. He fled up the verandah steps. Joey followed. He ran into the kitchen. Joey followed. He ran round the table, heading back out of the door, shouting 'Mem, Mem, Joey out! 'Joey stopped and sniffed. On the work surface was an opened tin of condensed milk.

My mother was in the dining room entertaining the Managing Director's wife to afternoon tea. Hearing the cook's cries she rose to see Joey waddle in, climb on to one of the chairs and upend the contents of the tin into her mouth. Sticky condensed milk dribbled down her fur.

'If only I was out of here?' thought the MD's wife.

'If only I had a camera?' thought my mother.

The label on the tin was 'Bear Brand Condensed Milk'! With a grunt and before my mother could stop her, Joey flung down her prize, headed for the door and was outside. With a bound she shinned up the nearest coconut tree. This wasn't her brightest idea as her collar got caught on the spiky leaves at the top!

Who would be brave enough to climb the very tall tree and dislodge a frightened bear which had huge teeth and rather lethal looking long claws? Joey was stuck up that tree quite a long time before a fairly puny, elderly, but agile Malay appeared and agreed to help her down. He slung a coil of rope over his shoulder, tying an end round his waist and securing a parang, a large curved knife on his back. Armed with a Mars Bar to distract her, he quickly kneed his way up the rough bark of the tree. As Joey reached for the chocolate, Ahmed looped an end of rope though her collar and cut away the restraining foliage. Now the hard bit was to encourage her down.

'Come on Joey!' shouted my mother coaxingly.

'OK', thought the bear . 'Been here too long!'

Scrambling down at speed ,Joey almost knocked her rescuer off his perch but, as he skilfully played out the rope, Mum was able to grab her as she reached the bottom. Giving Joey her gunny sack she led her back to the sleeping area of her enclosure. Joey's neck was bleeding from where the sharp spikes had caught her collar. After bathing the wound with salty water, Mum began to rub in an antiseptic ointment called Zambuk. Suddenly she noticed that the level of ointment seemed to be disappearing faster than she was using it. Joey was also dipping her paw into the tin and eating it!

Joey made a good recovery from her adventure. She was a delightful member of the family until my father moved from beautiful Ramunia to his new job at Nassau, in the Bahamas. There were more Scots there.

Joey was found a good home in the Sultan of Johore's zoo.

Poem by *Anita John*

The Gift of Life

To sing, in German, is *singen.*
Ich singe, ich sang ein Sang. I sing,
I sang a song.

When we saw the sign, in France,
le don de sang we read it to mean
the gift of song.

Later, we learned the truth —
blood donation – but the words
still sang.

For blood sings through the heart
and carries its own beat: lub dub,
lub dub, lub dub.

When blood sings, the voice sings
too, bringing light to itself
and others.

But when blood slows, thickens, thins,
or goes, the voice slows, stutters
and stops.

So break the song in your stride
take a seat and gift your blood
to the sac

so others might sing, the young
and not so young, so your gift
of blood might flow

into others, a gift of song,
un don de sang, ein Sang,
a song for life.

Tweed Elegy

Fiction by *Pamela Gordon Hoad*

When I close my eyes to remember home it's always the river I see first – even now. I see it sometimes under a cloudless sky, lapping serenely against its banks, or in muddy turbulence churning branches snatched from overhanging trees. It can be swollen by snow-melt from the high moors and a day or two later the waterfowl will be strutting awkwardly on tongues of exposed shingle in the middle of the sluggish flow.

So much of my old life was bound up with the Tweed. I splashed in the shallows with my mates, George and Davie, as we walked to the school-house, watching the salmon leap and the otters play. We learned to swim there and to clamber up the crumbling red cliffs where the channel narrows. I courted Annie in the long meadow where the oyster-catchers come from the sea to lay their eggs.

At first I tried to push the river from my thoughts because it wasn't just joyful memories it brought me. There were darker moments too: especially George's spitefulness, like the time he pulled the feathers off a dying duckling and chuckled as its squeaks faded into silence. He worked on a farm and seemed to resent Davie and me being apprenticed to a trade. He came to blows with Davie once over some footling argument and when their punches drew blood it splashed into the grass at the water's edge and a rusty stain eddied away in the stream. I should have realised then their rivalry would end badly. I should have had more sense than to get involved myself and let the bonny river bring my downfall.

During those long weeks we were on the ship I dared not think of the Tweed's pure water. In the stifling heat of that voyage pitch melted in the sun and while we sweltered and poured sweat we had to eke out a measly ration of putrid, lukewarm drinking water. There was sickness and death in the holds and some of the men were driven mad – others were downright bestial in their behaviour. At least the soldiers struck off our chains when we were out at sea and I was glad to get exercise scrubbing the decks, with my arms wet to the elbows. Landfall brought a wonderful improvement in conditions and I was lucky not to have come here twenty years ago when they say there was nothing but swamp and starvation for new arrivals at Botany Bay.

We were able to send a letter home to say we'd reached the settlement and I wrote to Annie. We'd been promised to wed in two years' time, when I was out of my apprenticeship. I gave her a bunch of ribbons as my pledge while we stood at the bend in the Tweed where the Duke's men wade out to fish. She blushed with embarrassment because she hadn't anything to give me. Then she knelt down and dabbled her fingers in the water.

'This'll do, Alex. The river's special to us and it can give us a token. With you being a stonemason, it's fitting.'

She held out a smooth white pebble, quite different from the darker stones round about, and the pleasure in her face took my breath away.

'I'll treasure it forever,' I whispered and I kissed it. Then I kissed her damp fingers and her laughing lips. We were so happy.

I knew I was lucky to have Annie. She was straightforward and loyal. George chanced his arm with all the girls, whether or not they'd got a fellow of their own. Some of them played along, gave him what he wanted and giggled about it afterwards, but Annie made clear she'd have no truck with him.

'Proper little puritan, you've got there,' he told me with obvious contempt.

'She'll keep you waiting 'til your wedding night, shouldn't wonder. Hope you're not disappointed then!'

I clenched my fists but kept my temper as I always did. I wouldn't pay him the compliment of being aggravated by his nonsense. Besides I knew the truth of the matter where Annie was concerned.

If only Davie had ignored such provocation but he let it rile him and was always trying to match everything George did. I told him it was foolish to set himself up as a rival and half of what George bragged about was invention. It didn't stop him though, more's the pity. George and his dad had always done a bit of poaching and the Duke's gamekeeper had his eye on them. When it was suspected salmon were being taken from the river the water-grieve buttonholed the three of us lads as we were skimming stones across the water. He frowned at Davie and me.

'You'd do well to choose your company more carefully,' he said, cocking an eyebrow towards George. 'I hope none of you'd be daft enough to break the law of the land. There's some already at risk of a severe penalty. Don't join their mischief. Part and art of a felony could cost you dear.'

We mocked his pompous words when he'd gone but we'd have been wise to heed them.

It was only a few weeks later that George got Davie and me to go with him to his Gran's cottage. He was full of himself that morning and we soon saw why, for there was the old woman slicing a new-baked salmon, as long as my forearm. He tapped his nose and winked. 'Just popped out on the bank, it did, round about midnight. No moon, you see, and the grieve was on a wild-goose chase upstream. We know they keep a watch on our house but they haven't troubled Gran since Gramps croaked. Have you ever seen such a monster? Bet you couldn't catch one like that, Davie Bunyan.'

I ground my teeth to hear George taunt poor Davie but I didn't think he'd see it as a challenge he had to accept. He was a decent lad. When he asked me to go with him to take a salmon I tried to talk him out of it but he was determined and there were tears in his eyes as he spoke of pulling

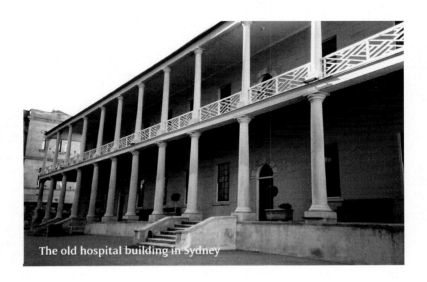
The old hospital building in Sydney

The Tweed

George off his pedestal for once. So friendship won and, against my better judgement, I went with him into the freezing water that blustery night. He was true to his word and he scooped up a fish with a skill that surprised me. It wasn't as big as George's but perfectly respectable and I was admiring it when the grieve's men charged out of the bushes. There must have been a dozen of them and we hadn't a chance but Davie lost his head and lashed out with his fists. Within hours we were lodged in Jedburgh Tolbooth, paraded before the sheriff and sent down to face judge and jury. I couldn't help but wonder if that ambush was simply a coincidence.

Davie had assaulted the Duke's official and he was shown no mercy. Like the grieve warned, I was found 'part and art' of the crime and sentenced to serve seven years: transported 'beyond seas', separated from everything and everyone I loved. Yet I was fortunate. On the morning I was taken south Davie mounted the scaffold in the Tolbooth yard and paid to the utmost for his bravado.

You could say my luck held after that. I survived the voyage and when I arrived in Sydney the new Governor was planning to turn the settlement into a proper town with fine buildings. Those of us with useful trades became ticket-of-leave men, let out of the penal colony to work on hospitals, barracks and churches, so long as we behaved ourselves. I never completed my indentures as an apprentice but I'm as experienced a stonemason as you'd find south of the Equator and in two years' time I'll have served my term and be a free man.

I'd released Annie from her promise while I was still in the Tolbooth but she'd have none of it. 'We'll still be young in seven years,' she wrote, 'young enough to wed and start a family. I'll wait for you.'

Some men decide to stay here when their sentence is up and there are good prospects for those with skills. I'd begun to wonder if Annie would come out to join me but I didn't want her to face that gruelling voyage and, besides, I was looking forward to walking with her by the Tweed once more. Then my sister's letter came and reality caught up with me.

'I'm sorry to write this, Alex, but Annie was always my friend and she's let me down but not as bad as she's failed you. She was married at Easter to that rogue George. I knew he'd been after her ever since you went but I was surprised to hear he'd got her in the family way. You're well rid of her.'

Those are not my thoughts but I can see many things clearly now. I was putting the finishing touches to the lintel over a church door yesterday and while they were mixing the mortar to fix it in position I made a notch in the side of the carved block, where no one would see it. Up there, tucked in behind the moulding, is a smooth white pebble from the bed of the Tweed, set above the doorway to a house of God which I shall never cross with Annie as my bride. Nor shall I ever see that dear old river again.

Music of the Spheres

Poem by *Carol Norris*

An echo – more than echo
And again a wave of sound
Propels through the still air
Wave after wave, the sea
Murmuring, the surf sighs
A memory in deep time
Lapping the shores
Of ancient lost Iapetus
His black ocean bed
White mountains now
From where this sound
Spinning by the rocks from far
To furthest horizon, dimly lit
By moonlight in the silent night.

Deep cold weighs down bright air,
Lifting harmony higher,
Ice begins to form and stealthy frost
Twinkles all along this valley
Desolate Ennerdale Head
In winter, roofless, is no place to be
Perhaps, or maybe the only place
To hear the music coming from the moon
Or Jupiter even – an echo from the
Music the earth sang at its creation.

Door to a different world

Non Fiction by *Dorothy Bruce*

A man stands waist deep in the river with a net. The tide is low and he digs around in the riverbed in search of something.

We ask Julia about it. Julia runs the little restaurant we dine in. From the outside its two mahogany double doors, white façade and ubiquitous promotional plastic tables and chairs, are unpretentious, and provide no inkling of the tastebud-tickling food served inside.

Initially we laughed at the paper stuck to the window that says the restaurant is recommended by Trip Advisor and Lonely Planet.

The locked door still amuses us. Never before have we come across a restaurant where entrance is by dint of a knock on the door and then a wait to be admitted, if the owner decides to admit you, that is.

Julia, the owner, escaped along with her large family from war-ravaged Angola in the 1970s, when she was eighteen months old. She busies herself with cutlery and condiments as if inherited memories and what she has learnt of violence in the country of her birth do not allow her to stand still lest she is overwhelmed. With a toss of her curly-haired head, she flicks irrelevant thoughts away and shifts conversation to the present and food.

Now her beaming smile says life is good. Her sister magicks dishes from ingredients in the kitchen while Julia serves and woos her customers, welcomes with a kiss on both cheeks, converses with them in their own language. Other members of Julia's family drift into the restaurant during the evening, to eat and help. Her family are important to her.

Diners acknowledge with a smile others who are admitted, chat across tables about where they spent the day, what they saw, their recommendations for your meal. In the small tile-decorated space some customers gabble Portuguese, some Spanish, many German, with a sprinkling of other languages including English, and our Scots. Some are locals, others are on holiday, a surprising number own second homes here, a place to escape to, where the sun can be enjoyed year round and frost never kills exotic plants or vegetation.

Such is the pull of sun and place that quite a few fellow diners fell head-long for the town and moved here to start up businesses. The openness with which they discuss the black market and black money surprises us. We are even provided with estimated growth figures. With the worsening of the economy, the black economy has flourished, fuelled perhaps by the raising of VAT from six to twenty three per cent for restaurants and pubs, a rise which when we were there was not being passed on to customers.

'When I came here the black economy was probably about ten per cent,' said a fellow diner who owned a pub. 'Now, it must be nearing fifty per cent.

Everyone's at it. That's how you survive.'

The good life for Julia did not come easily, but through long hours spent working in restaurants, watching and learning, engaging with customers. She's a savvy operator who knows her market, why customers come to her restaurant and how to keep them coming.

She has a daughter, a lively seven year old called Ana, who prances and dances around, theatrically pulls faces, declares, or stage whispers comments. She attends a small private school, likes the good life, takes it for granted, it's all she has known, though she is frank, carelessly so, about others close to her being less fortunate. She pulls a face, half an eye on her mother, when she blurts out her mother owns her aunt's house. Then she pirouettes off, away from her mother's frown, to amuse diners in another corner of the restaurant.

Julia's German husband was unable to find work in Portugal so returned to Germany. Julia could not settle in Germany and missed her family, so they live apart but phone one another every day.

In a nearby village further inland she has built a new house, and enjoys regaling us with tales of the snakes in her garden, of her neighbours still steeped in more traditional ways, their naked outdoor showering come dawn, and lifestyles led without electricity or modern amenities.

Such people as Julia's neighbours sell fruit and vegetables at the local market, a large modern, warehouse of a building on the edge of town. It is equipped with stalls complete with sinks and all that is necessary for the sale of fruit, vegetables, meat, fish, pulses, bread, flowers. Owned by the local council which, we were told, doesn't charge for the use of the facility, this is where smallholders from the surrounding area earn their precarious livings, while outside a thriving car boot sale takes place.

We bought bags of sea salt to take home as presents for the family. As well as being the area that provided the road salt required in plentiful amounts in Scotland during the winter of 2010/11, this part of the Algarve is also renowned for its epicurean sea salt for table use.

The salt pans that lie along the flat coastal area only operate in summer, but in March we watched as a few workers were building up the low walls between the pans, dredging up wet sand from the base with long wooden spoon-shaped paddles. In others a thin layer of crystals glistened on the sand, like froth on an incoming wave, remnants of the previous year's harvest. And presumably in search of food, in one flooded pan a pair of flamingos, heads submerged beneath the water, looked like fluffy three-legged bar stools.

'He was digging for clams,' says Julia of our man in the river. 'But not good. You must not eat them.' We remember unemployment in Portugal is over 15%. 'Now what you want this evening?'

As we take the edge from our appetite by nibbling bread spread with

sardine pate, we make inroads into a bowl of multi-coloured olives with a sheen like pearls, and study the menu. We remember the previous evening's fresh tuna, moist and bursting with flavour. A Portuguese dish but perhaps with a hint of Africa. The town where we are staying in the eastern Algarve used to be a tuna fishing town, now the Spaniards have taken over the fishing grounds, leaving, in the area's harbours, colourful little boats that catch mainly shellfish and octopus.

'I have something special tonight. Iberian black pig. Very good.'

A salad, piled high with grated carrot like glowing lava erupting from a volcano, appears. We'll want salad with the pig. Our culinary desires are fulfilled before even voiced.

It's my birthday and Julia has a cake tonight. Only occasionally does she offer desserts.

Then the brandy appears. Portuguese brandy, naturally. I rather enjoy it, though just as well our hotel entrance is next door.

As we leave we stroll across the limestone cobbled pavement and street to the riverside. We gaze at the Portuguese blue and red painted boats, hear, in the quiet of the evening, the plop and slap of water against wood and quay, admire the lights that streak the water with a kaleidoscope of colours. We turn to look at the very Portuguese façade of the restaurant building.

The doors of Julia's restaurant have opened the doors to a different world, its lifestyles, its tragedies, its hardships, its successes, its culture, its distinctive cuisine with a warm flavour of Africa.

The Welcome

Poem by *John Milligan*

Good Morning all, now let me see
We've Reid times two and Watson three
The Kerrs are four, with baby free
And Mrs Main
We've lost the group from Canonbie
But, Welcome to Spain

The first thing that I've got to say
Is how we plan to go away
Clear rooms at noon on your last day
For taxi at ten
You can change your clothes in the foyer
We do in Spain

Now, Mr Kerr, forget the order
Of pick-ups in the Southern Reporter
That didn't mention going to Forfar
And back again
Johnstons print beyond the Borders
But Here is Spain

Please get the Readers' Offer right
No mention of a scheduled flight
We're not responsible for the plight
It's not our plane
Your luggage should arrive tonight
Back in Spain

Now, not a single holiday passes
Without some little bruise or rashes
Be careful of the sewers and gases
And Mrs Main
We're sure to find your husband's ashes
Somewhere in Spain

But euros are the important things
For all your day trips, gifts and drinks
The club at night, it really zings
And coach and then
Don't forget the driver, kerching
We tip in Spain

Although the pool is in the brochure
And prominent in every picture
You'll find it's rather short on moisture
Completely drained
Waiting for a vital fixture
Not made in Spain

Ah, Mrs Reid, that top you're wearing
Although in Hawick might not be daring
Our Church defines that far too baring
Let me be plain
Cover your arms if you go praying
Here in Spain

The last thing that I've got to say
Is watch the food the first few days
Don't use the balconies, by the way
My name is Jane
I'm off to Venice for fourteen days
Welcome to Spain

Titian's *Man with a Glove*

Dorothy Alexander

Fictional Non Fiction by

Today, in her occasional column, writer and art enthusiast Lucia Longmuir meditates on her response to an early work by Titian*.

I was on holiday in Corsica, touring this spectacular, mountainous island, when I stayed for a few days in Ajaccio, its small provincial capital. My grandmother had died the previous month and this was my first chance to relax since this had happened. I was her only grandchild. Our love was mutual and uncomplicated. During her final illness I had spent some part of every day with her.

Ajaccio looks south and east across a magnificent bay to grey marled mountains that rise straight from the sea and fade to blue in the distance. The modest buildings of the old town are painted in shades of cream and terracotta. On the beach where Napoleon played as a boy, tourists and townspeople watch as Foreign Legionnaires, in all their physical splendour, take their daily swim just a short distance away from their headquarters whose honey-coloured walls dominate a rocky prominence on the town's waterfront.

For art lovers, Ajaccio's main attraction is the Musée Fesch, located down one of many delightful, traffic-free streets in the old town. It is housed in a palace built by Cardinal Fesch, Napoleon's step-uncle, who used his lucrative position to invest in large numbers of paintings, many looted by French armies in Holland, Italy and Germany. Its collection boasts such treasures as Botticelli's *Virgin and Child*, Veronese's *Leda and the Swan,* and Titian's 'smouldering' *Man with a Glove.*

As my taste tends towards the modern, I had little expectation other than that of satisfying my interest in looking at works of art accorded the label 'great' in the hope that, not for the first time, work from a period other than my preferred one would yield up its magic. And what magic there was to be had. Having given scant attention to walls full of religiose grandeur and floral or edible still-life, it was prurient curiosity that ensured my viewing of all rooms on Level 3 as here was displayed Veronese's *Leda and the Swan,* 'an uncompromisingly erotic work for its time'. But I found it curiously unsatisfying both in terms of its content and its execution. I turned to view the next exhibit, passing a window with a view across the sunwashed courtyard whose light seemed extra bright in the unlit room. And there before me was Titian's *Man with a Glove.*

How to describe the individual response to a work of art? For me, there are times when the emotional response becomes physical and tears well up, and this indeed happened in this instance. But there was something more. I can only say that it felt more akin to falling in love. I stood in front of this artefact, this thing of oil and canvas nearly 500 years old, and stared and kept on staring until it felt as if there was nothing else in the room, as if the painting had become my whole consciousness.

I have had similar experiences before: standing in front of a giant abstract by Mark Rothko, Miró's triptych *The Hope of a Condemned Man,* a tiny oil painting of a white rose by J.D. Fergusson. In such situations it is as if the painting resonates in some way, sensed by intuition, as if something intense enters through the eye and connects with the brain to give an emotional, even transcendental response which may bear no relation at all to the overt content of the work. It is as if the artist has answered Solzhenitsyn's plea, "Who will explain to mankind what is really terrible and unbearable, and what only irritates because it is near?..... Who could carry the understanding of this through the barrier of his own human experience?".

But the response had never before been so compelling. The painting itself was quite simple: the portrait of a young man dressed with restrained opulence in a black velvet jacket and a shirt of the softest white crêpe fastened at the neck with a silver hook and eye. His right hand was naked but for a ring of a dull red colour on his index finger. On his left hand he wore a glove fashioned in pale fine-textured leather with a deep cuff that had a V notched into it. Between the cuffs of his shirt and the glove, his wrist was exposed. He held the empty glove in this hand. Around his neck hung a long gold chain with a small oval pendant jewelled in the same dull red with dark blue and green stones at its centre. The colours of the background were deep and intense but harmonious; they seemed to merge with the outline of the jacket, with the youth's dark hair. From this sensuous density and splendour, the face emerged like a flower from its sepal. The features were fine. There was a small cleft in the slightly upturned chin. The eyes were dark grey and looked off to the left; there was pensiveness, a hint of sadness in their expression. The lips, exquisitely drawn, had a fragile, tender quality that implied a sense of anguished, impulsive inner life.

I did not want to leave this painting, to have to stop looking at those eyes, the gorgeous sensuality of those lips. The shroud-like quality of the young man's white shirt seemed to prefigure his own death. His expression, full of subtle grief, seemed full of the knowledge of the certainty of that death. And in that moment, I became everyone who has ever grieved by the body of a loved one and has had to tear themselves (or be torn) away.

Lucia Longmuir's latest collection of essays, Songs of Reintegration, *will be published by Void Press in May.*

*Tiziano Vecellio: 16th century artist whose innovations in portraiture and progressive dissolution of form into colour and light have continued to influence major artists up to the present day.

The light of the world

The light of the world
is not so unexpected.
It is here
rub the pane
let it in.

We only ever pray
for what we want
and not for what we need.

Russet and green the fallen leaves
collected coin upon
the late grown winter grass

White and black
frost fresh cut on tarmac
tracks the farmer's early rising

Blue and grey
chills ears and face
ghost wind over the land

Feel needy
and allow ourselves to pray
like the earth prays:

In spring for rain
In summer for sun
In autumn for the frosts
and then after the winds
in winter
it prays for peace.

Poem by *Christopher Ryan*

Deer Park

Suddenly, a wind whisper or a shadow figment
Across the long, end of season grass

A hint of a pause, a moment
Like this twilight rumour of rain.

Sleek heads turn in smooth abstraction
Disappear into the wooded dusk

Leave behind a sense of absence
The disturbed path's wildflower margin.

Outer Huntly

Here where tall pines endure
Is a view to Buccleuch's aristocratic pile
Standing high, grey, square and sure

Statement of power and intent
Less permanent our uncertain placed feet
Permitted tenant's shortest lease.

Across valleys of sleeping centuries green
On cue, ethereal shafts of sun break through
Painterly – more Tom Scott than Turneresque.

On this now deserted outback road
Beetles and slugs compete to be the blackest black
Flee the day's heat baked pheasant land

Seek dusk's deep wooded shade
Overhung by roosting rooks and crows.
We walk, we look, make tenuous human talk

Here where tall trees and clouds obscure
The slow windmill arms of distant change.

5th August 2011

In the Métro

Non Fiction by *Catriona Livingston*

It's going on six years since I returned to the Borders. Six years since I exchanged a daily one and a half hour commute underground, and the excitement of driving round the Rond Point de L'Arc de Triomphe, for the twisty scenic roads of the Borders. After twenty years living in a city, I appreciate the beauty of these roads more than ever; white van drivers excepted!

Nevertheless, my thoughts often return to these dark, endless Métro corridors which I navigated by radar for many years while my mind escaped to more interesting scenes and places. A fair part of my time was spent in wagons, or on station platforms, waiting for trains to arrive or leave. That was when I discovered the delights of people watching.

*****

The painter on a dingy platform caught, not my eye, but my ear. As he did his best to improve the look of the place with a touch of colourless paint, he sang. Favourites from Italian Opera, popular French songs, Duteil, Brel, Brassens. He didn't manage to improve the station walls but he did cheer more than one weary commuter. And I lingered to listen.

*****

One fellow in particular drew my attention. He would have been in his early thirties, grubby dark trousers, a grey sweat-shirt, tousled dark hair. He perched on a low wall on the station platform, apparently unaware of the crowds hurrying past. Commuters pushed and shoved their way in and out of the wagons. The January Sales had brought out the bargain hunters, and they contributed their weariness and aggressiveness to the usual stressful, rush hour traffic.

He was elsewhere. Spread out beside him on the wall, were the ingredients of a feast: a box of fresh oysters in their shells, a bottle of dry white wine and a Viennese loaf. Only the best for this underground diner! With the blade of his pocket knife, he prized open the shells and loosened the oysters from their beds. He threw back his head and let an oyster slide into his open

Page 89

mouth. He savoured the salty taste before taking a mouthful of wine. A chunk of the soft, tasty bread followed. Then another oyster. His pleasure in this underground meal was palpable. But I was left with a question which has pursued me ever since. Why? Why there? I could have asked him, but it seemed wrong to invade his privacy.

*****

It was unusual to have a journey on the Métro without someone telling the whole carriage a hard luck story, identical to that of the fellow before him. Sometimes we had to suffer a piece of music, more often than not, played badly. We became hardened to the constant demands for our attention and our cash. One rare day, the music was a treat and as I watched the musician and his interaction with the commuters, I found myself imagining what life was like for him, buried underground day after day.

*****

The dole queue until even the government's trickle of pennies dried up. Life, reduced to the basics: a bite to eat and a place to sleep. Glad I kept my saxophone, didn't sell it or pawn it. The time of a tune, I can escape. Seems I have a bit of talent. I also have my pride. Playing to earn a bit keeps that intact. It's tough though playing day after day to an audience that couldn't care less! Don't blame them really. They didn't ask to listen to jazz on the way to work.

What does me in are the ones that sit there enjoying the tunes and tapping their feet. Until I do a tour with my cap that is. Suddenly I'm Mr Invisible or they're in a hurry to go somewhere else. They won't even part with a few coins. Not them. They need every penny they've got to take the girlfriend out for a posh meal.

I've heard other fellows give them a mouthful, before moving on to the next carriage. Wouldn't do that myself. Gives us under-grounders a bad name. And I have my pride. Mustn't let them get to me. Need to keep my feelings under lock and key. Still it's hard to play your best for an audience of bent heads. These books and papers they're reading must be something else. Never seen such concentration!

There are really bad days! Days when the effort of playing is too much. Days when the cold cracks my lips or bronchitis makes me breathless, when people's faces are hard, and their expressions as dismal as the underground stations. Days when I feel like lashing out at all these heads, pretending to read. They're not deaf and I'm not a block of wood. I have feelings. Musicians, we're sensitive.

There are other days, frequent enough to keep me from topping myself. Someone gives me a smile, a thank you, a few coins, a cigarette, or even a luncheon voucher.

But there was one day when the sun shone right down underground.
A wee lad and his mother got on the train and sat down near me. He gave

my saxo and myself a good looking over, and then settled down to listen. Four years old and already a music lover. His feet, then his whole wee body started moving to the rhythm. Everyone could hear his loud whisper:

'He plays well, Maman, doesn't he?'

'Yes, dear.'

A minute or two later, a louder whisper:

'I like this music.'

Here and there throughout the carriage, smiles replaced frowns. I put my heart into the music - for the wee lad's sake.

'Oh, Maman, he plays well. Can I put some money in his hat?'

Around the carriage, hands went into pockets, purses appeared from handbags.

Rich pickings that day! Won't say I didn't need the money. But, what that wee fellow gave me, was what I needed even more…appreciation and respect.

*****

I miss these meetings with the many characters who inhabit the Métro. I am discovering though, that the Borders region has its own characters, equally worthy to figure in a future short story.

The Eiffel Tower

The Sacré Coeur

Summertime...travelling north

On the six o'clock clunking gingerly over North London points,
Through dark densely delineated houses with multi-faceted extensions
crowned with Mary Poppins' chimney stacks.
Now symbols of suburban joy -the bright lights and palaces of Tesco and
Big Mac,
Released now and bounding freely into the summer greenery.
Summer came in lazily, after the bruising of late spring gales,
But plays at being a proper summer with big bold sun and flawless sky.

We ghost through middle England, a land of make -believe that never was.
Moley and Ratty are stirring in the black Wild Wood.
Fields angling in perspective to the soft blue lost horizon .
In the many shades of green:
Apple, pea and tantalising olive...gray or green?

Suddenly vulgar excresences scar the sylvan scene - cynical concrete shapes
litter Milton's pastoral heritage, dancing in the checkered shade.
But...we do demand the power they bestow.
Compensatory fairy-tale houses in the early evening mists, shining
sugar white in comfortable safe farmland.
But a thought nags: where are all the brown 'n'white cows? Perhaps tucked
up in mystic byres?
Night is lurking so safe abed.

Newcastle's landmark bridges somewhat subdued in the closing dusk; a
steady marker on the journey home.
On again into the deepening northern night
under a half -hung irresolute sun curiously pale and flat casting the
first rose- wash on the hardening landscape.
A startling flash of birds, black and fast, low across the purple shadows;
Going where and why?
A lonesome distant tanker beetles its way along a curiously aquiescent A1;
another modern paradox.

Familiar satisfying shadowy coves appear, mysterious places with
crab-black silhouettes.
The placid seascape painted in delicate evening silver and ever changing
grays.

The long bend folds round and Berwick's stern castellated walls, safe
harbour, show firm and strong against the final night-bird sky,
And bridge us into a welcome journeys'end.

Travelogue

I have travelled far and travelled wide, he said.
Yet I have seen nothing and learned less;
Just joining up a pointless procession of dots on a flat -earth map.
I journeyed blinkered through the lands of the East,
And the social wilderness of Africa major,
Never seeing cruel poverty nor blinding social darkness.
Nor perceiving burgeoning new horizons of opportunity.
I blanked out the richness and flavour of multi-coloured, multicultural
worlds,
blind to all but pathetic myopic focus on my micro- world:
The way things were, should be, and shall be evermore...

So sad when playing back time's jerky travelogue,
To see at last what I should then have seen:
A golden panorama of mysteries and untold delights; but paradoxical
injustice.
Too late, then, for fresh discovery of peoples and their share of a brave
world,
Or the ever-widening gates of golden opportunity.
Not only have I lost a history,
I seem to have lost a life.

Non Fiction by *Jane Houston Green*

The Tempter

In Russian the word for 'painting' is pronounced phonetically as 'kartina'.

The noise of banging echoed throughout the train. I sat on the edge of the hard, narrow bed in the sleeping car trying to look composed with my knees together, back straight and hands clasped casually on my lap. Yet in grasping my passport who was I trying to fool? My heart thumped with every bang as the guards progressed down the corridors to me and my carefully wrapped white package lying in the luggage rack that, in protruding slightly over the edge, was clearly visible to all. The moment had arrived and whether my painting – my kartina – of the 'tempter' would make it back to Scotland hung in the balance.

'They are looking for bottles of drink and cigarettes.' I turned to look at my blonde haired German companion as she offered this explanation in French ... well, broken French, with gesticulations so I caught the drift of her meaning. We had managed to agree a language, down the track long beyond, and our teenage French had been the only common denominator with gesture and mime thrown in whenever necessary. It had made for some colourful exchanges.

'In the sides of the train ... the wooden sides ... they hide Vodka.' Hmmm! I could do with one of those right now. Or even a calming hot chocolate would suffice, from my friendly guard who had plied me with steaming mugs of frothy brown stuff ever since we left the platform at St Petersburg. Bless him! Perhaps my dear Russian friend, Volodia, had whispered in his ear as he always thought I needed looking after and that was fine by me but neither of these protecting men were anywhere to be seen in an acute hour of need. In truth, Volodia had prepared me with a strategy, after giving the bleakest scenario ... 'if they want they could throw you and the painting off the train'. The thought of being stuck at the border was somewhat alarming though this, he hastened to add, would be extremely unlikely. They would be more interested in money so could ask for an export tax on the painting and this would correlate to the original purchase price. Whether demanded in roubles or pounds really made little difference as I now had none of the former and very little of the latter ... grants from the British Council only go so far! If you cannot pay then they might just keep the painting but when they search the train you could just shrug, look innocent and say 'kartina' with a nonchalant air. They may well show no interest depending on what else occupies their day. Good point. Why should I be of significance? After all, I was simply an olive skinned English woman, a British citizen who lived in Scotland on a Russian train, at the Polish border, sharing a compartment with a French speaking German. What is not normal about that?

Why did I have to go into that particular art gallery and become haunted by this tempter? But I knew the answer ... the colours, the shapes, the boldness, the whispering ear, the coy glance, the design seeping from satin embossed gold waistcoat to sea-green spotted triangular hem. It was too expensive but it drew me in and enveloped my imagination so that the whispered words could almost have been ... 'she's hooked!' And I was, but with determined resolve headed towards the gallery door telling myself that there were more important financial demands and buying frivolous pictures was exactly that, frivolous. I went to the nearby banking establishment, but not into it, as the black market blatantly occupied the steps outside where young men with wads of roubles eagerly took pounds, dollars and any other currency deemed to have greater world market stability. And with that I left for the train back to the suburbs of St Petersburg and a wander through the busy supermarket where the shelves emptied more rapidly than they were stocked.

Over supper I told Volodia, and his wife Sasha, about the picture expecting them to think I was slightly mad to even contemplate such a purchase. Surprisingly they showed a calm interest and this perplexed me until I realised that they were pleased by my keen appreciation of their culture and moreover, understood that actors are often inspired by other art forms even if, with low and erratic incomes, they can rarely afford to buy them. While we sat at the small wooden table, set under the window in their compact kitchen, talk wandered as it did most evenings to other topics and issues. We were never shy to include love, religion, politics and with such open exchanges seconds became minutes that turned to long hours and, in turn, many a night slowly whittled away.

Mornings were a different matter but the Maly theatre beckoned and would be obeyed with a regime almost as strict as any preconceived expectation of communist Russia. The world had changed by 1992 but deep down the power struggles continued so any challenges could easily escalate and fear was only slowly being chased away. After informative hours with the voice instructor and a session of singing Russian folk songs I was allowed to escape for a few hours ... ignore the dry rot on the stairs ... past the subway with its deeply dug platform decorated by ballroom chandeliers ... round the corner by the arch and on to Nevsky Prospekt ... the main street in St Petersburg. Now I could enjoy the ambience, cultivate acquaintances and walk past my art gallery! The sun shone in a clear blue sky enhancing the colours of the painted buildings, where bullet holes still awaited repair, and the roofs of ornate orthodox steeples glinted invitingly. It was October and while I had packed many a cosy jumper and thought of vital layering with additional hats, scarves and gloves aplenty it was all unnecessary. St Petersburg was basking in an Indian summer ... not for me the fate of Napoleonic armies or German Nazis ... no, my trip was more

The Tempter

about Neapolitan ice cream and nasty tarmac smells with huge rolling machines making the road noisily pristine. It was all glorious!

A few days later I sat in the darkened theatre with the ever searching eye of artistic director, Lev Dodin, hovering nearby and watched rehearsals of Broken Jug by Heinrich von Kleist. I could empathise with the dancing sequence as we had been learning the steps in class but soon a debate began about the actual jug being used and the props team were sent to search for another ... and another ... and yet another! The momentum of the morning had dissipated so I crept out to find Volodia and together we disappeared past the rumbling road machinery to a coffee shop that was robustly atmospheric and served divine pastries. We enjoyed eating and neither of us worried about the calories ... particularly Volodia who was tall, broadly thin and angular. His straight hair hung down and framed the chiselled features of his face but the overall effect was one of disturbing gauntness. Feeding him was a treat!

Soundly full of cake, coffee and chat we left to visit my painting. Volodia was also enamoured and explained that the title literally meant 'The Tempter' ... we chuckled about that for a while until we could no longer hide behind other framed hangings without giving some justification to our existence. He knew the artist was beginning to attract attention and gain respect in relevant circles so it would also be a good investment. Negotiations ensued while I listened to the rhythm of the language as with the rapid conversation there was little for me to grasp with any understanding. After various gesticulations and curious facial expressions Volodia bustled me out of the gallery and down the street to those familiar bank steps where we changed my last fifty pound note. Not long after that productive transaction we were travelling home on the metro with a rather large framed canvas wrapped in metres of white plastic. Beneath the muttered burbling and clamour of people bustling through their lives I could almost hear the whispered approval of my tempter and see, in agreement, a slight nod with raised eyebrow from his feminine companion.

'Passport'. Recollections disappeared as I looked up to see a guard, intimidating and immaculately dressed in uniform, standing over me. His outstretched hand demanded my identity document which I meekly passed for perusal and, having flicked through the pages to verify that the photographic image matched my reality, he handed it back before turning his attention to my carriage companion. As he did so he noticed the over burdened luggage rack but said nothing. Moments later he looked back at me ... glanced, once again, at the large white package ... scowled into my eyes ... accepted my mumbles of inept Russian phrases ... and was gone. I listened intently as his footsteps disappeared down the corridor of the train and, with every step making a return improbable, breathing became an easier task.

Shortly afterwards creaks and groans of wooden panels combined with clanks and rumbles of metal tracks signified the train preparing to gather momentum ... slowly through the Polish border ... and then rapidly as we began to speed towards the final station of East Berlin. Passing through mile upon mile of countryside there was nothing unique about the views and, while Autumn might be waiting to move, only leafy deciduous trees and lush green grass could be seen thorough every grime-edged carriage window. The scene had a universal familiarity that was strangely comforting.

Perhaps I needed that comfort in some deep part of my soul as I have never returned to St Petersburg nor seen again any of those friends and acquaintances though I have thought of them often and wished them quietly well. My kartina has travelled further afield, frequently being packaged and unwrapped, as I have stumbled from one experience to another making homes wherever time and opportunity has allowed. With hanging pins placed my tempter, and his lady, have looked out from many a wall and the bold designs, in a palette of rainbows, still remain as bright and exciting as the memories from which they arrived.

Beyond Mosspaul

February 5th 2012

The season is coming around again.
Under the rise and bend of frosted skies –
Spring's dutiful and habitual growth.
By rutted fields, steam puffs from isolate homes
folk reside in this their only span time
of short personal happiness, boredom and disgruntlements
village hall dance and satellite TV cannot dispel
and after Mosspaul, fresh powder snow
wedding cake slice, iced meringue hills
ghost thought and feeling mythologise
signpost the way to a Queen's Hermitage
prose South to Langholm and Grieve's Republic.

But where Ewes Water flows - affirmation of faiths
familiar wind over cold pebble and stone
persistent, permanent stoical friend
murmured promise of yesterday fulfilled
this is its valley where it must abide
on and on, nowhere else to go
subject to Earth's gravity, the pull of slope
a binding of near eternity?
Where will they build the border post?

Poem by *Julian Colton*

Paradise

Palm trees. Wherever one looks, palm trees are rife in this vortex of paradise. Bundled boughs of green and yellow blades hang their heads and buffet in the whispering breeze. Beyond the boughs, sits the almost daily blue carpet, brightened by the rays emanating from the source of all life. The orangey-yellow fireball hides in the shade of a cloud, the only cloud visible on this day.

Pre-historic looking, ravenous 'whopper' birds, fill their bulging beaks with squirmy, gasping fish, their wet feathers glistening in the sunlight. They soar in gangs looking to do as their leader, yet look more for moments to escape and swoop down, so that the shadows in the waves may transmute into flesh for another meal.

Tiny, thin, hollow, bony, shelled fingers with pathetic, protruding spikes poke themselves out from what appears to the eye to be, a flawless silky sheen. Yet, as if stabbed by a pair of rogue dressmaker's scissors, the sheen shatters and clumps of random sandy clusters appear strewn over the golden patch. The clawed fingers heave up an almost transparent excuse for a body and scuttle over the grains looking for food or shelter. Oh to be of an innocence to see such a sight and still be titillated by the speed of such insignificant yet fascinating life forms. Watched and chased by predatory gulls, the creature realises the only escape route is back down. Its quest for a meal or cover will wait until later.

Time stands still when the grey-blue fins rise, swerve, curve and systematically and gracefully carve their way through the wet, rippling waves. A stillness and beauty most would love to last forever. There's always something going on, wherever you look there is something beautiful, a natural force, a mammal or animal creation at play. It's like turning the street corner in Rome for further abundance of an ancient mural, mosaic or church, each with its own, unique story to tell.

It's paradise, so why ever say goodbye? Could there be such a place where all is well as it seems, where one can wake up and breathe the air of life into one's lungs, knowing a free and wondrous day lies ahead?

It was not quite three years before a family landed back from the vortex of paradise to UK shores. The once known paradise suddenly became a memory, the once reality disappeared from view like the curtain closing at the end of a Broadway show. Here and now, in the Borders, the curtains would be drawn to embrace an unknown and alternative kind of day. Waking up to find barely adequate clothing, just enough to brave the rays, suddenly became a thing of the past. It was now about how many layers could they fit under their jacket with a lining? It was as if their own toes were

Non Fiction by *Hayley M. Emberey*

sobbing. So used to only have to contend with sandal straps, their toes were now muted and muffled by thick cotton or woollen blankets, living in darkness covered by hard, cold boots, rather than living in a liberated fashion in the glowing light of day.

Rolling, green, hilly mounds endlessly merging one into another sat rooted around this family. The colour green had never shown off so many different shades to the eye. Abundant were the textured trees and bushes that tweaked the horizon. Placed sporadically on the green patchwork quilt, cream and black, fluffy balls, bleated and chomped incessantly. Babies nestled into the warmth of their mother's jumpers, their fate unknown – further bounding in the fields, wiggly tails a' waggling, or plated up for a traditional haggis meal?

Around corners of long, winding lanes, presided vast estates and castles of architectural beauty, set back amongst the picturesque scenery. Their solid presence with a stillness like that of a guard watching over all who entered, oozed history, generations' worth — stories of conflict, love, joy, tragedy, birth, life and death.

Pea-brain male pheasants with magical colours meandered aimlessly in the direction of oncoming vehicles, or fell victim to the local farmer's bullet frenzy. Water was abundantly prevalent, teaming with life to be admired or caught and served up for supper.

The family could live with this. The air spoke a different language here. It was paradise in a way that only the heart could sense. All was well as it seemed. Time stood still with very little going on, at times for ages or for miles.

But fancy if both places became one? A place where the sun shone more but there was never a shortage of water; the dolphins leapt with the salmon; the sheep and cattle hung out with the mountain lions and bears; the pelicans soared with the buzzards; the palm trees mixed in with the heather providing shade for the bag-piping surfer who told the crowd, 'Awesome, I found a coo in me hoose last night!' and the local Standard Bearer announced to a crowd of lifeguards on the local beach, 'There's fresh, organic Bubblyjock in town out West for Thanksgiving you know!' A place where plum and apple trees grew amongst orange, lemon and avocado orchards and vineyards; where folk danced 'Flamenco' and 'The Dashing White Sergeant' to Chumash musicians and violinists.

Paradise.

The Stranger

Non Fiction by *Dougie Morrison*

He came from a different culture
I wondered if he would be a dove or a vulture
He greeted me with head bowed and hands clasped
I extended my palm and this he grasped.

We spoke a few words and ordered a beer
He told me how he liked it here
Friendly people and the justice of law
He told me he had left a land at war

Nepal invaded by the armed Chinese
Crossed the border and did as they pleased
Subjugate the Buddhist manna
Talked of exiled Dalai Lama

To return one day is what he hopes
To his land of mountainous slopes
He sees his god from all around
In the trees, rivers and on all ground

We chatted over the beery brew
And he told me of places he had been and knew
Through India he escaped
Crossing through wooded landscapes

From Asia to Europe he fled
A refugee it must be said
He worked his way through the continent
Living in a makeshift tent

Until he arrived on these shores
Where he settled to run no more
He now toils in a Scottish Borders town
In peace and quiet he goes around

Far, now, from a country in disorder
He lives in peace in the Scottish Borders

Doubly perchance

A stroll through life...

An after dinner stroll seemed such a good idea. The breeze stirred the light muslin in a lazy way, inviting action; enticing one outside. Stirring in rhythm with the curtain I arose and meandered out into the heavy summer afternoon. Nothing mattered, nothing raised the energy to fire a cerebral neurone.

Distant thunder clouds threatened, but so, so far, far away as if to have no relevance to the life in this garden.

Slowly slipping through the wicket gate into the lane as though a languid movement from a stream into a river into a pool.

The lane, green lined, at first with beech, at first with green, soft green; then slowly as eyes explored, seeking cool shadows; as senses adjusted, seeking shades of emotion as hunger for detail insinuates into the brain; only then did the purples of the hawthorn intrude, giving way to the poisonous blue of the nightshade or the thrust of the contrasting cuckoo-spit.

The gaps in the hedge caused a jolt. No, not a gate, an old hunt jump. Witness to loud pony clubbed girls, cheekily trumping chinless wonders; toppling from tippling tipples of hunt cups; scarlet in face and back, black in mood and silk, contrasting with impish children on mud spattered ponies; manes tied in ribbons, tails garlanded with bows.

The breeze intruded again, chasing the barley across the field. Wave upon wave, nausea on nausea until almost dizzy from watching I wandered on again.

The breeze stiffer now, disturbing mind and birds and leaves. Corn buntings flashing across the way bracketing a lark high in the blue azure sky, forcing a gaze upwards, like urchins at a Guy Fawkes display or squaddies watching a Very light high above no-man's land. A hiatus, action or no action, a question; a pause and dissipation, the mind lapsed back into the heavy warmth of the afternoon.

How far to walk? A destination seemed poetic; a quest - the mind wandering again. The old elm tree on the hillside seemed enchanting. A sole survivor of the wars; only Dutch not German. Greens contrasting with greens, shimmering as breezes caught themselves in the branches, as twigs crossed swords and shed the shadow's blood across their baize.

Perhaps too far, perhaps another younger day, perhaps a Pimms beckoned with its multifarious sparkle refreshing eyes and palate alike; flickering memories of parties and guests, posh and old; light and gay, from a time when the world understood that word. A time of gentleness of colour, of levity, where had it all gone?

Yes indeed, time to go back, time to seek the blue grey shadows of the home hiding behind the stark bleached white washed walls. Perhaps, perhaps time for a nap. Time perhaps to go elsewhere..... Time.....

Perchance
a short poem

A thought
Lives
Spirals
Weaves
And dies

It's ripple
Sometimes felt
throughout one's life
Or touching others
lives on....

Such a parcel o' rogues

Non Fiction by *Russell Bruce*

These familiar words from Burns' ballad *Fareweel to a' our Scottish fame* are much quoted and a perennial favourite in collections of Scottish folk music. There must be few nations, if any, without its rogues so there is no merit in this being a Scottish distinction. The context for Burns was the Union and the enabling siller that got the resolution passed to adjourn the old Scottish Parliament in 1707. Wherever there is money, power sits in its shadow and the commonweal at risk from rogues attracted to the honeypot.

The last two lines of Burns' poem
> *"We're bought and sold for English gold :*
> *Such a parcel of rogues in a nation!"*

is an internalised expression of angst that masks in some ways the difficulties of the period and the influence of a powerful neighbour after Jamie the Saxt had moved south for a better job where the wishes of monarchs were less contested by a troublesome and querulous population. Foreign policy moved south with Jamie as Burns dryly notes in another song *There'll never be peace till Jamie comes hame.* Markets and trading relations with Scotland's pre Union of the Crowns allies were closing for Scotland as they differed from those of England for historical reasons not unconnected to the strife of previous centuries between the two countries. Yet trade with English colonies remained a closed door. Jamie coming hame was a forlorn expectation.

The rogues in today's society whether Scots or of any another nation involved in the international banking meltdown has interesting parallels with Scottish and English affairs in the years before and after the Union of the Parliaments. Locked out of trade with English colonies had ensured closer economic collaboration between the nations did not progress, the Scots looked to establish a colony of their own on the unclaimed coast of the Isthmus of Panama. William Paterson a wealthy merchant and banker from Dumfriesshire founded The Bank of England in 1694. In 1695 he returned to Scotland and succeeded in persuading the Scottish Parliament to pass an Act for the creation of The Company of Scotland, granting the company a monopoly to trade to India, Africa and the Americas. Another Act of the Scottish Parliament in that year facilitated the setting up of The Bank of Scotland with a monopoly for a period of 21 years.

The outcome of the ill-fated Darien Scheme is well known but the machinations contributing, in part, to its failure less so. It did not suit English foreign policy to upset the Spanish who had colonies in adjacent territories to the Isthmus: "Despite the ships docking at Montserrat for supplies, they were refused both water and food by the Governor acting under instructions received from England to the effect that the Darien Colony was illegal." (Ms, 1685). Relations with Scotland were not improved by the Aliens Act of 1705 which would result in all Scots, except those resident in England, being treated as aliens and exports from Scotland of coal, linen and cattle would be suspended.

Intended to force negotiations for a Union of the Parliaments it was a clumsy threat aimed at limiting Scots ambitions to open up independent trading routes. William III's war with France had in the 1690's severely disrupted Scottish mercantile trade and illegal English naval policing of Scottish waters had resulted in the Scottish Parliament commissioning three warships to counteract this interference. Opposition to a Parliamentary Union was also evident in English politics. As Tom Devine records, in 1700 the Tory leader in the Commons claimed Scotland was a beggar and '*whoever married a beggar could only expect a louse for her portion*'.

Patterson's dream of a Free Port in Darien to open up a new trading route to benefit from growing trade with the East was over. With the last of the Stuarts, Queen Anne, now the monarch of both countries and whose unwise support of the Aliens Act implemented by the Tories but repealed later that year (1705) by the new Whig government, the Union of the Crowns was in a perilous position. The matter had already come to a head in 1703 when the Scottish Parliament passed an Act of Security establishing the power to approve a separate Scottish monarch to succeed Anne unless trade with English colonies was opened up to Scotland.

A critical stage had been reached and Queen Anne's determination and that of her government to effect a Union of the Parliaments looked unpromising. For the Scots there were other considerations not least England's high level of debt that would become a joint liability. The Scottish Government had no debt but Scottish investors in The Company of Scotland had lost their investment. At the time subscriptions were being raised there was a great deal of interest in London where investors saw opportunity in a new trading company to break the monopoly of the English East India Company. London financiers helped raise over £300,000 in 1685. This free movement of capital would establish Scotland as a serious competitor to England's trading interests. The London Parliament threatened legal sanctions against London merchants who invested in the Scottish enterprise. The funds melted away and the London book was closed. Despite both The Company of Scotland and The Bank of Scotland competing for subscriptions at the same time, having both been established by Acts of the Scottish Parliament in 1685, Scotland raised the capital. In February 1686 a new subscription to raise £400,000 sterling for The Company of Scotland was opened and subscribed within six months. As Professor Devine says 'it was a remarkable achievement'. The competition with the fledgling Bank of Scotland to raise capital in Scotland would have been expected to raise interest rates but in fact interest rates fell.

The Articles of the Act of Union of 1707 set out the financial settlement to Scotland amounting to £398,085 and ten shillings which apart from a small proportion to settle arrears of salary due to office-holders, effectively swapped private debt to the tune of nearly £400,000 as represented by the capital of The Company of Scotland on which 5% interest was to be paid as compensation for assuming liability for a share of England's debt: *'which, according to the Agreements aforesaid, may become payable to Scotland, by way of Equivalent, for what that Kingdom shall hereafter become liable, towards Payment of the Debts of England:'* (Article XV).

The Articles of Union also dealt at some length with the harmonisation of customs and excise duties with some respite period before some English taxes were to be introduced in Scotland. The introduction of the English Salt Tax and later the Malt Tax, introduced in 1725 aroused great anger in Scotland. Smuggling was endemic, although by no means confined to Scotland, but the House of Commons was incensed at the lack of taxes contributed from Scotland and the ineffectiveness of Customs and Excise north of the Border. Scots for their part argued that they had never had such an onerous tax regime and that they were being forced to pay for England's ever rising levels of national debt. In 1770 English nation debt amounted £60.58 million, by the time of the Union it had risen to £62.13 million and UK debt quadrupled to £242.36 million by the end of the eighteenth century. Over 300 years UK national debt rose year on year and millions became billions.

An account of the enormous difference in the cost of basic products as a result of taxes introduced following the Union is amply demonstrated by the displays in the smuggler's mansion, Gunsgreen House in Eyemouth, designed by Robert Adam and now run by a local charitable trust.

In the meantime the shareholders of The Company of Scotland had decided to leave the Equivalent settlement of £389,000 with the English government in return for an annuity of £10,000 and were quietly salting away these funds. By 1727 the Equivalent Proprietors were operating as bankers and obtained a charter in the name of the Scottish Banking Company, later to become the Royal Bank of Scotland. This helped rescue the reputation of William Patterson who was a brilliant financial innovator but badly miscalculated the supporting forces required and the political obstacles stacked against his dream of Port St. Andrew on the Isthmus of Panama. It is an irony of history that this strategically important part of Central America might have had massively beneficial outcomes for the trade of both nations and a 'better together' precedent had William III responded to the Scots request for the support of The King of England.

Another Scot with a colourful history was also a pioneer in the development of banking. John Law, born in Edinburgh was the son of a family of bankers and goldsmiths. A banker and economist, he promoted the theory that paper money could be backed by the value of land.

Law had moved to London in the late seventeenth century. Challenged to a duel in 1694, it is said, over the affections of Elizabeth Villiers, Countess of Orkney, Law ran the hapless Edward 'Beau' Wilson though with a single thrust of his sword. Law was arrested, tried for murder and sentenced to death, later commuted to a fine for manslaughter. Wilson's relatives appealed but Law escaped and thought it prudent to move to the continent. Elizabeth Villiers is otherwise remembered as the acknowledged mistress of William III.

Law was in Scotland in 1705 advocating to the Scottish Parliament the establishment of a land bank in which notes would be payable in land instead of bullion. Law had set out his theories on money supply, value and return on trade in his treatise Money and Trade Consider'd with a Proposal for Supplying the Nation with Money. Referring to the Bank of Scotland's issue of notes to four or five times the value of cash held, Law said that was a clear addition to the money of the nation. It was more national than either the Bank of England or that of Amsterdam, because "*its Notes passing in most payments, and through the whole country: The Bank of Amsterdam being only for that Town, and that of England is of little use but in London.*"

His national land bank plan was rejected in Scotland and his ideas for expanding credit when bullion was in short supply were not to come to fruition until he established the Banque Générale in France in 1715. Appointed as Controller General of Finances, Law set about a series of reforms in the wake of the economic damage caused by Louis XIV's wars. He broke up large land-holdings to give the peasants land, abolished tolls on roads and canals, encouraged the building of new roads and started new industries. Within two years output increased 60% and France's merchant navy grew from 16 ships to over 300.

He may have become a hero, had not his consolidation of the trading companies in Louisiana into The Mississippi Company, not resulted in the 'Mississippi Bubble' bringing about the collapse of Banque Générale. Law fled France disguised as a woman and died in Venice. Law was a brilliant mathematician and his reputation has been reassessed for his contribution to the development of modern commercial banking and national economic management. What our society has yet to master is to spot the gambler in bankers like John Law. Law was known to win card games by mentally calculating the odds.

In Scotland the rivalry between the Bank of Scotland and The Royal Bank of Scotland, often vicious in the seventeenth century, continued into the twenty-first. In 2000 The Royal Bank beat the rival bid from Bank of Scotand for Nat West. For both banks, that was to lead to subsequent events that brought them both to the brink of collapse within a space of just eight years as the international meltdown in the banking system ripped its way across the globe.

Burns might have said *'such a parcel o' rogues in the warld!'*

References
Articles of Union 1707
Devine, T.M. (2004) Scotland's Empire 1600 -1851, London, Penguin
Ferguson, W (1968) Scotland: 1689 to the Present, Edinburgh, Oliver & Boyd
Graham, W. (1886) The One Pound Note in the rise and progress of banking in Scotland and its Adaptability to England, Edinburgh, James Thin
Law, J. (1705) Money and Trade Consider'd with a Proposal for Supplying the Nation with Money. Edinburgh, Andrew Anderson
Robertson J.L. (1923) The Poetical Works of Robert Burns, Oxford, OUP
Spenser Collection, Ms Gen 1685, Special Collections, University of Glasgow

Author Biographies

Dorothy Alexander is a writer and creative writing tutor who lives in Galashiels. For more information please see - www.dorothyalexander.co.uk

Gunther Alexander is difficult to define, currently working as a Chartered Accountant with a previous career as an Engineer with numerous patents to his credit, writing is definitely not the main career move but rather a latent itch coming to fruition.

Dorothy Bruce – short-listed in a number of short story competitions including the Scottish Wave of Change competition. Workshops run by Treading the Borders Theatre Company have encouraged her to write plays. Blog - http://jingsandthings.wordpress.com

Russell Bruce writes for online news services. He has worked in publishing and advertising and was for 8 years a board member of Loch Lomond and The Trossachs National Park.

Tom Bryan - born in Canada but long-resident in Scotland, living now in Kelso. Widely published and broadcast poet, fiction and non-fiction writer. He was the first editor of The Eildon Tree and a founding member of the Borders Writers Forum.

Iona Carroll - writes mainly short stories and novels. Occasionally getting published! Writes reviews for New Books and other publications. Now one of the editors of The Eildon Tree magazine. Also conducts workshops for writers in the Borders.

Antony Chessell is a graduate of London University and the Open University and is a retired Chartered Surveyor. His recent books include Coldstream Building Snippets and The Braw Trees of Coldstream and his next publication will also have a local theme.

Gwen Chessell's first publications were in the field of medical education. She now writes about nineteenth century worthies, preferably with medical/naval connections, and has had two historical biographies published.

Pim Claridge - Writing since childhood, Pim's poetry, from the heart, paints landscapes of many countries, achieving both publication and acclaim. Reading for Charity brings her work to an even wider and appreciative audience. 'a free spirit, she writes as an artist paints'.

Julian Colton's poetry publications include Something for the Weekend (Scottish Borders Council, 2001), Two Che Guevaras (Scottish Borders Council, 2007) and Everyman Street (Smokestack Publishing, 2009). He has also published a book of children's ghost stories, The Looking Glass Years (Scottish Borders Council, 2004). In 2008 he was CREATE writing fellow for Dumfries and Galloway Council. He co-edits The Eildon Tree magazine.

Marie-Claire Dibbern is a Borders based writer and playwright. She has had her work showcased by the Traverse Theatre and came runner up in the Rowan Tree Theatre Company's 21st anniversary playwriting competition with her Borders inspired entry 'The Ferry Man.'

Oliver Eade – (www.olivereade.co.uk): Retired doctor. Publications 30+ short stories, four children's novels; awaiting publication, teenage and adult novels. Play, The Gap, short-listed for Rowan Tree Competition 2009.

Hayley M. Emberey - Wherever you go in the world you take yourself with you and preferably a pen and paper. Hayley's been doing just that since she was 27 years old after a personal awakening into self-realisation and healing. Her writing journey is about to launch into a more public domain through children's and adults stories, fiction and non-fiction with an underlying emphasis always on who we really are and why we are really here, wherever we are in the world.

Vee Freir Vee Freir is a Clinical Psychologist who moved to the Borders four years ago from the Highlands. Since moving writing, and particularly writing poetry, has become an important part of her life. She recently had a poem published in The Eildon Tree.

Pamela Gordon was chief executive of two English local authorities and held a number of public appointments. She now sits on various committees and writes historical fiction

Lynne Henderson – After recently completing an honours degree in Literature and Art History with the Open University, Lynne went on the do a two year diploma with the OU in Creative Writing.

Jane Houston Green is a professional actor and part of a large extended family. She is also Artistic Director of Treading The Borders Theatre Company and writes creatively whenever she can grab the time!

Fiona Hunt lives in Peebles, Scottish Borders and enjoys cycling, hill-walking and playing 3 musical instruments, but never simultaneously! A creativity workshop at the age of 50 prompted her to start exploring latent writing skills, heavily influenced by her hobbies and nature.

Anita John is a creative writing graduate from Edinburgh University and tutors for its Lifelong Learning Department. She is one of five poets selected for the HappenStance/Writers' Forum Mentoring Scheme and most recently won the 2012 Biscuit Combo Prize. See www.biscuitpublishing.com/.

Bridget Khursheed - Bridget Khursheed is a British-Australian poet and geek based in the Scottish Borders (poetandgeek.com). Good on mountains, bad on towers.

Robert Leach, has published three collections of poetry, a number of pamphlets and the epic, The Journey to Mount Kailash. Among his other books are theatre histories and a double biography of John Arden and Margaretta D'Arcy, Partners of the Imagination. Robert's wife –
Joy Parker is a painter and sculptor with a WASPS studio in Selkirk. Her most recent solo exhibition was 'In View of India' in March-April 2012 at the Sam Scorer Gallery in Lincoln.

Catriona Livingston - Born and brought up in Selkirk, Nursing Training took her to Edinburgh. Midwifery in Bellshill followed. In 1969, she moved to France where she spent the next thirty-seven years in bookshop management. Retirement brought her back to Selkirk where she writes short stories for her own pleasure.

John Milligan - Born 1940, my remote and primitive cottage life stimulates a comprehensive negation of post-polio syndrome and inspires prizewinning Scots poetry and songwriting but this supra-Borders vein has actuated a piece in English.

Dougie Morrison – born in Glasgow and moved to Galashiels many years ago, and enjoys writing about whatever he sees, hears or experiences in life.

Pat Mosel is an experienced journalist and writer, born in Zimbabwe and now living in the Scottish Borders. Visit www.patmosel.co.uk

Tom Murray is a playwright, widely published poet and fiction writer. His prize winning play Sins of the Father was toured by Rowan Tree Theatre Company autumn 2011. He is currently Creative Writing Fellow to Tyne and Esk Writers based across Midlothian and East Lothian. His website is - www.tommurray.org

Carol Norris – Grew up in Nottinghamshire near to that part of Sherwood Forest which remains. Has lived in the Borders since 1984. Recently co-opted as third Editor on The Eildon Tree magazine.

Arthur Parsons Arthur Parsons writes poems and plays. He is particularly interested in co-working with Theatre Groups, musicians and a-capella choirs.

Ronnie Price's interest in writing was inspired by a schoolmaster who encouraged active creative writing of prose and poetry instead of learning chunks of 'literature by heart'. First books published were 'sexy thrillers set in formula one scenery'. Latest book is non-fiction motor racing history. Most enjoyed authors: PG Wodehouse, Ian Fleming, Raymond Chandler, Dornford Yates and Peter Cheyney – and some high quality erotic writing.

Christopher Ryan - came to the Borders from Australia in 1973. Freelance writer and poet, cafe and bookshop owner, and a director of the Chisholme Institute near Hawick, his first novel, 'The Story of the Damascus Drum' was published in 2011.

Rosalie Saunders, nee Brydon - Born Selkirk. Spent some of her childhood in Malaya, Worked as a Midwife in India. Is trying to write her memoirs before she is deid!

Raghu Shukla - India-born, ex-Consultant Physician NHS, senior editor of an internationally contributed book on elderly care (1996), short story in CANDIS (1989), Handbook for Writers (awaiting publication). His writings reflect human resilience as well as vulnerability, and Indian connections.

Margaret Skea - Hawthornden Fellow and award winning short story writer – recent credits include Neil Gunn 2011, Chrysalis Prize 2010, Winchester Prize 2009, shortlisted for Mslexia 2012 and long-listed for Matthew Pritchard Award, Fish Short Story and Fish One Page Prize. Published in a range of magazines and anthologies in Britain and the USA.
Her debut novel Turn of the Tide was the Historical Fiction Winner in the 2011 Harper Collins / Alan Titchmarsh People's Novelist Competition and will be published in November by Capercaillie Books.

Eileen Thornton - has been writing short stories and articles since 2001. Her debut novel, The Trojan Project, was published in 2008. She is a member of several writing organisations, including The Society of Authors. A selection of her published work is displayed on her Website - www.eileenthornton.co.uk

Photographic/Illustration Credits

All Photographs are copyright

Page	Title	Copyright
Title	Tibetan mother (section)	Gunther Alexander
4	Costume at The Haining, Selkirk	Dorothy Bruce
6	The Olivers	Russell Bruce
7	Eyemouth Harbour	Arthur Parsons
12	Boatman	Joy Parker
13	Asha	Joy Parker
16	Border hedge	Lynne Henderson
21	Spanish Dancers	Oliver Eade
22	Neidpath Viaduct	Fiona Hunt
25	Wallace statue, Beymerside	Russell Bruce
29	Kuala Lumpur	Pim Claridge
30	*Domestic Medicine* title page	Gwen Chessell
34	Scottish Coat of Arms, Melrose Abbey	Dougie Morrison
34	Union of the Crowns, Galashiels	Dougie Morrison
35	Union of Parliaments, Berwick	Dougie Morrison
36	Hizzy	Christopher Ryan
39	The Leet Water	Antony Chessell
41	Venice	Arthur Parsons
47	Statue of Ganesha, South India	Jay Shukla
50	St Cuthbert's Church Celtic cross (1)	Ember Hall
50	St Cuthbert's Church Celtic cross (2)	Ember Hall
55	Tibetan Hills	Gunther Alexander
58	Mother, baby, horse	Gunther Alexander
58	Prayer flags	Gunther Alexander
62	Model of SS Doric	Carol Norris
68	Berwick-upon-Tweed	Phil Thornton
69	Berwick Bridges	Russell Bruce
70	Quilts, Drakkensberg mountains	Pim Claridge
70	A viewpoint called God's Window	Pim Claridge
77	The old hospital building, Sydney	Pamela Gordon Hoad
77	The Tweed	Pamela Gordon Hoad
82	Man in river, Tavira, Portugal	Dorothy Bruce
82	In the salt pans, Tavira, Portugal	Dorothy Bruce
82	Houses by the river, Tavira, Portugal	Dorothy Bruce
84	Holiday rep	John Milligan
89	Notre Dame church, Paris	Catriona Livingston
91	Eifel Tower and statue of Liberté, Paris	Catriona Livingston
91	The Sacré Coeur, Paris	Catriona Livingston
93	Berwick Walls	Dorothy Bruce
96	The Tempter	Jane Houston Green
109	Bank of Scotland note of 1723	Russell Bruce
Cover	Gunsgreen House with Chinese junk	Dorothy Bruce

Back cover – sections of images from pps 96, 58, 12 and 82 as above